A Concise Guide to Energy in the United Kingdom

A Concise Guide to Energy in the United Kingdom

Sponsored by Genersys plc

Published by Genersys plc

First Published 2002

© Copyright Genersys plc

Genersys plc
92 New Cavendish Street, London W1W 6XJ, United Kingdom

We have endeavoured to state the facts, as they are known to us
as at 31st December 2001. The views and opinions expressed
herein are those of Genersys plc, its directors and staff.

British Library Cataloguing-in-Publication Data
A catalogue record for this book is available from the
British Library

ISBN 0-9543232-0-3

Produced by Bookchase (UK) Ltd, 2002
Designed by Chris Fayers
Jacket design by Gary Hicks
Additional research by Martie Newton
Printed and bound in Great Britain by Biddles Ltd. *www.biddles.co.uk*

Contents

Foreword

We at Genersys are proud to have commissioned this book. It contains not only the important facts about energy in our country today but it also sets out the views of our directors, salespeople, technicians and scientists. Some of the issues it deals with will make you feel uncomfortable and concerned for the future, but we can also point the way to some of the solutions.

We take a pragmatic view; it is essential that we act to cut down on pollution and by that slow down the rate of global warming. We must all do it – consumers, whose consumption is a critical part of the problem, government, local authorities, industry, commerce and the international community.

Our own existing installations are growing tremendously each year. We are grateful to our customers for their confidence, foresight and trust in bringing this about.

With our manufacturing partner ThermoSolar, our hard working sales, technical and administration teams, and believing in an ever increasing awareness of the issues by the public, we aim to install more than one million square metres of collectors by the end of the decade, that will bring clean 'green' energy to hundreds of thousands of people.

Douglas Dalziel
Director, Genersys plc,
Bristol, July 2002

Introduction

Poor countries use less energy than rich ones. Rich countries waste more energy than poor countries. It used to be thought that as energy use increased so a country became more prosperous. But energy use based upon indiscriminate burning of fossil fuel has proved wasteful and harmful. With fossil fuel shortages and supply difficulties the rich countries regarded nuclear power as the solution.

In 1974 I attended the NATO conference organised in Odeillo in France on behalf of Dornier, who were later acquired by DaimlerBenz. The conference was entitled "the Challenge of the Energy Crisis." Many countries arrived at the conference with impressive solar energy experience. The United States had started a variety of solar projects. Israel and Australia had fledgling solar industries. In Germany Dornier had designed a solar desalination plant that it planned to build in Jordan. Greece had built solar greenhouse and desalination plants.

The main focus of the conference was not environmental. People were not then aware of environmental issues as they are today. The NATO nations were worried about interruptions to the supply of oil and price increases; in Britain there was industrial unrest in the coal industry. These were the problems that we thought we faced, not the problems of global warming.

Over the next twenty-five years solar technology developed. I am proud to have been part of that development. There are now systems that provide reliable and continuous performance. As the cost of fossil-based energy inevitably increases, in terms of money and human misery, solar power must be the answer. Clearly oil reserves are limited and sooner or later all governments will be forced to impose higher energy taxes. Continued fossil fuel burning is simply not sustainable.

The following chapters outline the possibilities, advantages, and disadvantages of energy sources and technologies. It is hard to reach any conclusion except that in the medium term the adoption of solar collectors by households and industry will make a highly significant improvement to both our prosperity and our environment.

The solar collectors produced by Genersys are the result of scientific and engineering discoveries by people from Britain, France and Germany. Of these, in recent years, German engineering has developed the product but it now falls to British ingenuity and British entrepreneurial expertise to develop the markets and make the technology available throughout the English-speaking world.

Peter Schubert PhD,
Markdorf, Germany

Chapter 1

Our energy needs

We all need energy to keep warm, to heat and clean our homes, and to warm the water that keeps our clothes and ourselves clean. When we work we need energy to light our workplaces and power our tools whether they be lathes or computers. We use energy to get us to work and to help us buy our necessities and luxuries. We need energy for our hospitals and for our entertainment. We get most of our energy in the form of gas, electricity and petrol.

So, an essential function of all governments is to ensure that there is a supply of plentiful, cheap and accessible energy that is secure and cannot easily be disrupted. This is as important a part of a government's responsibility as defence, law and order, medical services and education. Without energy our lives would be substantially impoverished and at greater risk.

In modern times energy policy has been directed to ensuring a diversity of supply so as to prevent one industry or group of interests, like, for example, the British coal industry unions in the early 1970s, or other states and countries, like OPEC behaved in the mid 1970s, from having an undue influence over the United Kingdom by being able to cut off the energy supply. Most of our electricity and petrol comes from gas and oil that in turn comes from huge multinational corporations. Governments must ensure that these corporations do not have excessive power over any state. These corporations are very large and deal in essential products so it is quite easy for them to have, by their sheer size, undue influence without any sinister motives.

Generally most countries have tried to cope with these problems by ensuring that they have a diversity of supply. In the United Kingdom the electricity generating industry was originally dominated by coal but then diversified into gas, oil and nuclear power generating stations. Coal gas was replaced by the natural gas that came with the fortunate discovery of oil and gas in commercial quantities in the North Sea.

By the early 1990s the United Kingdom had plenty of energy. A policy of privatisation meant that there were a number of suppliers of energy in each field. Competition meant some control on prices. People used more energy and use of energy grew and grew.

While energy use expanded there also grew a more and more widespread concern about the effect of its increasing use. More people acquired cars as public transport systems declined or became too expensive or too dangerous; cars were more often than not the cheapest and most convenient way to travel. Cars cause pollution in an obvious way that everyone who stands next to a busy major road can experience. But increased use of energy within residential or business premises also causes pollution, when we burn fuel in order to generate electricity or to heat our homes and work places. This pollution is not as obvious as traffic fumes or smoke billowing from factories but is just as dangerous.

We all consume energy in the form of electricity, gas, oil and other fuel in almost every aspect of our lives from when we wake up in the morning and turn on the light until we go to sleep at night. Even then energy is being consumed within our homes and outside them for our benefit. There is street lighting, energy used by hospitals and the emergency services and energy used by night workers in baking our bread or making other products that we need.

Modern life inevitably involves many journeys: to work, school and on social occasions. Families no longer invariably live and work close to each other in small communities. While thirty or forty years ago most journeys would have been by public transport, people today value the safety, cleanliness and convenience of driving around in their cars. Other factors of modern life conspire to make the car essential for most families.

Housewives of forty years ago shopped almost every day for food but working people today are just too busy to be able to shop daily. Instead they have to buy larger and heavier volumes of shopping. Usually, this means a trip to a supermarket by car. Much of what they buy is needlessly packaged, requiring cars to carry the increased weight and more waste-disposal vehicles to remove it to larger infill sites.

People often expect (or are prepared) to take their children on long journeys to what they perceive to be a better school than the local one. They go on more frequent weekend breaks, fly abroad on holidays and they shop at hours convenient to them at places which are almost inaccessible if they have to use buses and trains. It comes therefore as no surprise that transport is the major energy user.

The amount of energy used for road freight and road passengers per mile of distance travelled has remained fairly constant over the past 25 years, but the huge increase in energy used for transport can be attributed to the large increases in distance now travelled by both passengers and freight and, in particular, the increase in the number of cars on the road. A family car was once a rarity. Nowadays two and three car families are common.

Energy consumption by households for heating water and space, and for cleaning and preparation of food has also gradually increased over the past twenty-five years so that over that whole period it has risen by 21%. Although there are fluctuations from year to year – due to some winters being colder and some summers being hotter – the general trend of domestic consumption of energy is upwards. We expect this trend to continue. The overall growth in energy consumption is thought to be largely due to the increased number of households, rather than individual households using more energy, although we believe that over the next twenty years energy consumption will also increase within each household.

We expect that people will continue to bath and wash more and use more exotic forms of lighting – internally as well as externally for security purposes. More family members will have and use their own individual televisions, music playing equipment, computers, and other electrical equipment. We are no longer one TV families.

While energy consumption has increased significantly over the past 25 years this increase has taken place against the background of very large energy efficiencies that have disguised the true amount of energy-related activity increases.

During the past 25 years the biggest waste of household energy – poor loft insulation – has been addressed in many buildings. In 1974 only 40% of the housing stock had loft insulation and then the average insulation was only one inch thick. By 1998 almost all housing had loft insulation, most of it being of a reasonable depth to insulate the loft well.

Hot water storage cylinders were also poorly insulated 25 years ago, but modern insulated cylinders have replaced most old cylinders. In addition many households have installed double-glazing. While this is not suitable for all housing, there is no doubt that once installed it does bring energy efficiencies, although it is not as effective in saving energy as a well-insulated loft and a well-lagged cylinder.

Although energy saving by insulation has had a discernable effect on energy consumption, overall it has not done more than compensate for the increased use of energy by new appliances and more frequently used machines.

There are also savings in energy consumption that have been made and no doubt will continue to be made by energy efficient white goods. These include fridges, washing machines and tumble dryers where the savings are probably close to optimum. As far as space and water heating are concerned, the development of energy efficient boilers – such as the condenser boiler – can lead to great savings but they are expensive and not suitable for all installations. The government scheme for a £200 refund on the purchase of a condenser boiler was phased out in April 2000 but the government still levy value added tax on condenser boilers and on insulation.

Savings from insulation and energy efficient appliances are modest. We expect more consumption of energy over the next 20 years as life-style demands and increased prosperity create desires in households to, for example, install air conditioning, heated swimming pools and similar facilities that will create an increase in the amount of energy consumed by each household. There will also be predictable increases in consumption of energy caused by population growth, particularly in the undeveloped and developing worlds.

It is worthwhile examining in some detail exactly how the average household uses the energy it buys before we can consider how we can use less energy. It is important, however, to bear in mind that these figures of energy consumption within households do not reflect one critical point. The energy lost in transformation of fuel and delivering is greater than all the energy consumed in the home. So when you consider the amount of energy that a household uses, it is not just the consumption registered on its meters that should be considered but also the huge, unavoidable losses of energy involved in getting the supply into the home that must be taken into account.

First, we shall look at the overall picture. In 1970 domestic households used the equivalent of 37 million tonnes of oil for energy (that is how the government measures these things). Of this 21 million tonnes (57%) was used for space heating, 10 million tonnes (27%)

for water heating, 3 million tonnes (8%) for cooking and another 3 million tonnes (8%) for lighting and other appliances.

By 1997 overall consumption was 44 million tonnes. Of this 57% was still used for space heating, 27% for water heating, 4% for cooking and another 12% for lighting and other appliances. It appears that when you consider these proportions and take into account energy efficiency savings by insulation generally, households are living more comfortably and luxuriously than they were in 1970. More people keep their houses warmer and use more hot water. They could wear more clothes and wash less, but they do not.

We should approach these figures with some degree of understanding. This is particularly important when considering hot water usage. The stark figure of 27% of energy in the home being used for water heating includes a great many very small households comprising one or two people. In fact, we believe that an average family with two children of school age probably spends around 35 to 40% of its energy expenditure in heating water for household use. A single person household probably spends less than 20%. These figures include bathing, washing, clothes cleaning and general household cleaning water. Households with more than two children – say three adults and two children or two adults and three children probably spend more than 40% and larger families will spend appreciably more than 40% on their hot water.

Most people will find the base figure of 27% (including as it does an average with single person households) very surprising. If you add to that the cost in environmental terms of the energy lost in creating and transmitting the power that heats the water, it is surprising that there is still no significant use of the sun in the United Kingdom as a source of free hot water.

Against this background, space and water heating systems have changed. In 1970 only 30% of the housing stock in the UK had central heating. Of those houses that were centrally heated most were heated by coal. By 1998, 89% of the housing stock was centrally heated. Of that 89%, four out of every five houses were heated by natural gas.

Over the same period domestic household appliances used 85% more electricity, the greatest increase coming from more people having fridges, freezers, washing machines and tumble dryers and using them more frequently.

For all these improvements, between four and a half and five million households in England (not the United Kingdom as a whole) spend more than 10% of their income on fuel, even though in real terms energy prices have been falling for the past ten years. This is a shockingly high figure, which only addresses actual expenditure. It must be reasonable to assume that the figure required to achieve a decent standard of warmth must be higher than 10% of income in a good many of these four or five million households, the vast majority of which or consist of our elderly poor.

Households in the United Kingdom consume 29% of all the energy the United Kingdom creates. Transport consumes 34% and industry only 22%. Where does all this energy come from?

Chapter 2

Our energy sources

Traditionally most of our energy came from coal. Our wealth was founded upon coal. In 1970, only 30 years ago and well within the lifetime of most people living in the United Kingdom today, the country produced over 147 million metric tonnes of coal, according to Department of Environment figures. Half of this was burnt in power stations and the heat was used to generate electricity, while significant amounts of coal were still burned in the home for space heating.

Apart from clean air legislation, there was little in the way of environmental protection from the by-products of coal burning, which included not only smoke, carbon dioxide and carbon monoxide, but also other harmful acids that were released into the atmosphere causing acidity in our rivers and lakes.

Within 25 years our coal production had fallen to 48 million tonnes. The vast majority of current production is now used in power stations, but in 1998 power stations burned about two thirds of the coal they burned in 1970. Our coal production has fallen by over a third, but imported coal is extensively used. We have saved money by closing down most of our coal mines and making those in the mining industry redundant, replacing the coal we no longer mine with imported coal mined in other countries. Today, three quarters of the coal consumed in the United Kingdom is used for generating electricity.

In 1999 the Government officially estimated coal reserves at existing coal mines at about 200 million tonnes. These reserves would last for only five years at the current rate of extraction, so that by 2004 it would seem that our coal industry will no longer exist.

Coal production is influenced by international prices. They have fallen slightly in the past two years. There is also a demand for better quality coal producing fewer pollutants. Most official bodies, including the European Commission, foresee a further decline in the coal market over the coming years. All European coal is now very expensive to produce, compared with imported coal. Although coal production in the European Community in 1998 was about 107 million tonnes, production is reducing year by year at a rate of about 15 million tonnes a year. As European Community production falls so imports of coal into the Community will increase.

At one time we talked derisively about "taking coal to Newcastle" because the North East had plenty of coal. Now we are taking coal to Newcastle from Poland, Columbia, South Africa and even Australia and Indonesia.

The European Commission forecasts that coal imports will actually decrease by about 5% annually – which reflects an overall trend in the United Kingdom and the rest of the European Community to burn less and less coal. We expect this trend to continue and that the environmental costs of coal burning, discussed later, will ultimately prove to be too high for any reversal in this trend.

Natural gas is an important fuel in the home, in industry and for generating electricity. In 1970 we produced 11.1 billion cubic metres of natural gas – less than half of 1% of our probable and provable reserves of gas at that time. Within twenty-five years we were producing nearly 70 billion cubic metres a year – which was just about 4.45% of our reserves.

30% of natural gas is burned to generate electricity in our power stations but households directly consume 35%. They burn gas in their boilers for space heating and hot water.

The definitions of our gas (and oil) reserves are important. The government defines proven reserves as known reserves which have a better than 90% chance of being produced, probable reserves are known reserves which are not yet proven but which are estimated to have a greater than 50% chance of being technically and economically producible. The government's estimate of proven, probable and possible gas reserves is actually increasing year on year notwithstanding the fact that we have extracted over one trillion cubic metres of gas over the past 20 years.

Natural gas has wholly replaced coal gas, that is to say, gas produced from coal. There is a sophisticated network of supply pipes throughout most of the country and the vast majority of households have access to piped natural gas. Northern Ireland at present has no natural gas although there are plans to connect it to the mainland gas network. For those households, particularly in rural areas, who do not have access to piped natural gas, there is liquid petroleum gas and calor gas that can be delivered to storage tanks at the home. Sophisticated remote monitoring devices enable gas tanks to be filled without the consumer having to make a telephone call; the supply is now virtually as seamless as a piped supply.

Oil is also a very important source of fuel. When the oil companies started to drill in the North Sea forty or so years ago they hoped to discover oil. They did find oil, but natural gas discoveries proved to be probably more important than the oil they found. Nevertheless they found enough oil to make the United Kingdom an oil producing country in the space of a very few years and although oil was always an important source of energy, the fact that the UK produced sizeable quantities of its own oil enabled the energy producing industry to be less dependent on volatile regions of the world for its oil.

In 1970 we produced very little oil – less than 160,000 metric tonnes – a tiny fraction of our reserves. Within 25 years we were producing 126 million tonnes of oil a year. This amounts to 7.8% of our reserves each year. Oil refineries have always produced more than the country demanded. The actual quantity of product refined has remained relatively unchanged from about 1986 onwards.

The United Kingdom will be self-sufficient in oil and gas for several years to come. For the past 20 years this country has consistently estimated each year that its proven, probable and possible oil reserves stand at around 2 billion tonnes. In that same 20-year period we have extracted about 2 billion tonnes of oil so that as we extract we discover new supplies. If the price of oil is low, then the cost of extraction can be uneconomic. Increases in oil prices can make what were unviable oil reserves worth exploiting.

The UK government believes that reserves will still be discovered and that we can continue our present level of production for much longer than a decade.

Another major source of the power we consume is nuclear energy. There are over a dozen nuclear power generating plants in the United Kingdom and the generation of electricity by nuclear power started as early as the mid 1950s. The United Kingdom Atomic Energy Authority's figures show that the nuclear industry has grown into a major electricity generating force. By 1997 nuclear power generated 26% of our country's electricity production, compared with 33% for coal and 29% for gas.

There are, of course, other installations, but British Nuclear Fuels owns and operates eight Magnox nuclear power stations in West Cumbria, Southern Scotland, Essex, Kent, Somerset, Avon, Suffolk and in Anglesey.

Calder Hall in West Cumbria was the world's first commercial scale nuclear power station and was officially opened in 1956. It now generates enough electricity to supply Leeds. Between them, the Magnox power stations alone provide around 8% of the UK's electricity.

Properly designed and maintained nuclear generating stations produce electricity without producing emissions. Indeed, the lack of carbon dioxide, carbon monoxide, smoke and other emissions is an important factor in favour of nuclear power stations. Nuclear power does not create by-products of smoke, carbons and noxious gases. It is probably the cleanest form of power but it is not without considerable disadvantages. Were it not for the problems of safety and radioactive waste, nuclear energy would be an almost ideal source of power. Relatively small quantities of uranium are needed to generate huge amounts of electricity.

Renewable sources of energy are becoming increasingly necessary. Renewables include solar, hydropower, geothermal, wind and biomass energy; the latter includes energy generated from other renewable sources such as coppicing, straw and similar fuels.

Renewable sources of electricity generation in the United Kingdom account for only a tiny proportion of the total amount of generating capacity. These sources are mostly hydroelectric schemes. The natural gentle contours of most of the United Kingdom do not lend themselves to producing more hydroelectricity than we produce at present.

The actual figure for renewable sources of electricity generation in the United Kingdom in 1988 was only 3% of the total amount of generating capacity – a modest 1.5 gigawatts.

Ultimately the energy in falling water derives from the sun – hydro-electric energy is another form of solar power. Energy contained in sunlight evaporates water from the oceans and deposits it on land in the form of rain. Differences in elevation result in rainfall run off and thus allow some of the solar energy to be converted into hydroelectric power.

Falling water has been used as a power source for thousands of years: water powered clocks in ancient times and then mills to grind corn and for other applications. In 1882 moving water was used to power a waterwheel on the Fox River, Wisconsin, and electricity was generated. Shortly after the Fox River experiment proved the viability of hydroelectric power, the first of many generating plants was built at Niagara Falls.

Early hydroelectric plants were very reliable and more efficient than the oil and coal fuelled plants of the day. As the price of oil and coal fell, and electricity demand soared, small hydro plants fell out of favour. Most new plants were huge and involved major dams.

These dams flooded vast areas of land. This in itself causes humanitarian and environmental concerns. Until recently most people believed hydroelectric power to be safe, clean and environmentally positive. There is no emission of carbon dioxide or sulphur dioxide and there is no risk of radioactive contamination.

However, some studies reveal that large reservoirs created by flooding do produce harmful greenhouse gases. The decaying vegetation under the water, produces, it is believed, the same sort of quantities of greenhouse gases as those produced from other sources of electricity.

By 1999 capacity from renewable sources in the United Kingdom had increased to 3 gigawatts. Whereas the other sources of generation typically use 50% of capacity on average, the average capacity use of renewables, is about 80%.

The figures include so-called "bio-renewables" such as wood, straw and other fossil based fuels, which can involve pollution. They also include free sources such as wind, waves and the sun. It is here that we can discern the beginnings of what we hope will be the trend for the foreseeable future, that is, the generation of electricity by using the wind and the producer of wind power – the limitless power of the sun.

But for the time being, in order to produce most of our current, we must continue to use and probably increase the number of our power stations and their capacities, unless by using the virtually limitless energy of the sun we can each acquire our own private source of free power now.

Chapter 3

Energy and atmospheric pollution

As we began to use energy in increasingly large amounts concerned voices began to be raised about the increased pollution. Some people pointed out that acid rain was poisoning our rivers and lakes. Others claimed that the use of fossil fuel could be linked to holes appearing at the North and South poles in the ozone layer of the atmosphere. Many eminent people warned that the globe might be becoming warmer and warmer and that climate change would cause irreversible damage to our environment and ultimately to ourselves.

The human being is a reasonably sturdy animal; he (or she) can live in both cold and warm climates. But the temperature range in which humans can actually live is only a tiny fraction of the range of temperature that it is possible for our planet to experience.

Quite apart from all these factors our own experience seems to indicate, in a completely unscientific way, that there is truth in these warnings. It seems to us that more children suffer from asthma these days, that the sun burns our skin more quickly than before, our weather is more unpredictable and the seasons less reliable than in earlier times. Weather conditions in these temperate isles are becoming more extreme. Summers are hotter or wetter and autumn brings hurricanes and tornadoes instead of gales. In the year 2000 there was extensive flooding not only in coastal areas but also as a result of riverbanks bursting under the pressure of too much water. Homes built on land that had never previously flooded were badly damaged by floodwaters, not once but twice in some cases. These extreme conditions are harmful, unhealthy and wasteful.

If our instincts reflect the scientific truth that there is something wrong with our weather then we do not need to search for causes – they are obvious. Instead, we must examine our use and consumption of energy and their impact on the environment.

As we have seen, our main sources of energy are coal, oil and natural gas. A large part of these fuels is converted into the electricity that is our major form of power. The burning of these fossil fuels generates much of our electricity in the United Kingdom. The use of nuclear energy does not necessitate the burning of fossil fuels. A separate process creates heat. However, the key point to remember is that every time you use electricity – by making a phone call, washing your hands, turning on a light, watching television or making a cup of tea – you either burn fossil fuel or you create nuclear waste – unless you have your own "green" power station.

The basic principle that applies to all traditional power stations is that water is heated into steam by burning fossil fuels: the steam drives turbines, which generate electricity. By-products include steam, heat, gases and fuel waste. In order to generate electricity from coal, oil, gas or even nuclear fuel, the process involves heating water into steam. The steam passes through turbines, turning them, which in turn produces electric current. By this simple process current is created in the same way as current generated by a small bicycle dynamo, which can power a bike lamp, as long as the rider is turning it.

Because electricity is so important in every aspect of our lives, it is essential to have sufficient plants capable of generating current to meet all possible requirements within the country. Demand for electricity varies enormously throughout the seasons as well as through the course of a twenty four hour period; huge surges of power are needed, say, after the end of a popular television programme when people start switching on lights and kettles and cooking. The need for power on a hot summer's day is different from the requirement on a cold winter's evening, so making sure that we have enough power is not always a simple task.

We can monitor whether we are generating enough current by calculating how much of their capacity electricity generators are using in terms of how many total hours they could have run. This is called the "plant load factor". In 1970 the plant load factor stood at 40% - the generators were using less than half their potential capacity. In 1998 this had risen to 53% but the most current ever required during 1998 never required the generators to produce more than 82% of their possible capacity.

In addition to burning fuel to create electricity, we burn oil in the forms of petrol, diesel and domestic heating oil, which is usually kerosene. For the past 10 years oil refineries have always produced more than the country demanded. The actual quantity of product refined has remained relatively unchanged from about 1986 onwards, although it fell by 29% between 1980 and 1985. We also burn natural gas for space heating, water heating and cooking.

When we generate electricity by burning fossil fuels, indeed whenever we burn fossil fuels, we create and distribute atmospheric pollutants, the main ones being *Blacksmoke, Carbon Dioxide (CO_2) and Carbon Monoxide, Nitrogen Oxides and Sulphur Dioxide (SO_2)*. We shall examine each of these pollutants that we have been, and still are, pouring into the air in increasing quantities.

Blacksmoke is suspended solid matter that is produced when fossil fuels, such as coal and oil, are burnt. Because the combustion of these fuels is almost always incomplete, the unburnt solid matter is suspended in the air, soiling buildings and causing the haze which reduces visibility in fine weather. Most of the blacksmoke in our towns and cities comes from the combustion of diesel fuels. Particles of blacksmoke that are less than 10 microns in size have been linked to fatal respiratory diseases. The smaller the particle size, the more deeply it penetrates our lungs, often with terrible results.

Asthma sufferers will be very aware of the discomfort they have to endure caused by blacksmoke. A significant proportion of blacksmoke is caused by fossil fuels used in generating electricity, but most is caused by people's use of heat and transport directly. In 1993, 5% of blacksmoke was created by energy production, private households accounted for 34% and transport for 27%. If private households burning fossil fuels (coal and oil mainly) were to reduce their dependence on fossil fuels for their hot water systems by using solar collectors, then we estimate that the blacksmoke emitted in the UK would fall by at least 10%, creating a measurable and significant contribution to cleaner air and a healthier nation.

Carbon Dioxide is created every time fossil fuel is burnt and every time living organisms breathe out. Plants use the carbon dioxide that all life forms exhale in the process called photosynthesis. Plants absorb carbon and emit oxygen. In this way plants clean the air and keep the carbon dioxide levels low.

Carbon dioxide is a long-lived pollutant, remaining in the atmosphere for between 50 and 200 years. It contributes significantly to the Greenhouse Effect, but it can be converted by photosynthesis in plants back to oxygen and plant material. Sadly, the equatorial rain forests, a great source of CO_2 absorption, are being rapidly destroyed.

It is thought that there have been natural fluctuations in CO_2 levels in the atmosphere. In the Holocene period, the past 11,000 years, CO_2 levels have varied enormously, according to studies from the Scripps Institute of Oceanography, San Diego, and the University of Bern. By taking core samples of Antarctic ice and analysing the air bubbles for CO_2 content Scripps found that 11,000 years ago CO_2 was present at the rate of 286 parts per million by volume (ppmv) of air compared with about 190 ppmv 18,000 years ago and 285 ppmv in the late 1700s. The present rate is 364 ppmv. That is significantly the highest concentration that has been measured. This research supports the view that changes in CO_2 levels prompt changes in temperature, which in turn increase the CO_2 levels in the air. We shall deal with this later when we consider global warming.

In the UK private households are responsible for the production of 22% of carbon dioxide (not to mention the production of 77% of carbon monoxide) according to government statistics. Clearly, these emissions would be significantly reduced if households adopted solar power for their water heating needs.

Emissions of CO_2 from burning fossil fuels have actually decreased in the United Kingdom over the past 25 years. On the United Nations basis of measurement we emitted 19% less CO_2 in 1998 than we did in 1970 but 7% less in 1997 than we did in 1999! Emissions from transport, with engines burning more cleanly, fell by 39% between 1980 and 1998. Emissions from power stations, the largest single source, also fell greatly during this period but now appear to have levelled off. The United Nations calculates that during that time we discharged 149 million tonnes of carbon, in the form of carbon dioxide, into the atmosphere. However, others put the figure as high as 156 million tonnes.

If electricity is generated from natural gas instead of coal, half the amount of CO_2 per unit of energy generated is produced. Nuclear-powered generators do not produce CO_2, neither do hydroelectric generators. These forms of generation do have potential adverse environmental consequences however – either in the form of dangerous by-products in the case of nuclear energy, or damage to wildlife in the case of hydroelectric power.

It can be hard to picture the damage that can be done on a nation-wide scale by carbon emissions. Figures often fail to bring home the facts in a way that we can understand, so it is helpful to reduce these cold statistics down to what they mean in terms of individual households.

We have calculated CO_2 emissions saved over an average year by an average household using solar collectors. If we assume that the solar collectors are operating at average efficiency, being used only for top up water heating with average performance, in a household using gas to heat water, then the household will emit *700 kilograms of CO_2 less each year than an identical household not using solar collectors*; if the household was using an oil fired system the savings in CO_2 would be about 20% greater still. If the solar collectors were also used for basic space heating then the saving is more than an extra *700 kilograms of CO_2* each year. 700 kilograms of carbon dioxide is equivalent to one thousand litres of soot. That is a very large bag of soot indeed, and that represents only one year's production by an average household.

Over the 35-year life span of the solar collectors, 24,871 kilograms of carbon dioxide will *not* be emitted into the atmosphere. If the collectors are used for space heating as well as water heating at least a further 24,000 kilograms of carbon dioxide will *not* be created. All of these emissions (and more) will be created by an identical household in the United Kingdom without solar collectors. Now we are talking in terms of truckloads of soot.

Although, as we have explained, carbon dioxide is absorbed by plants, they cannot absorb all of the emissions that now take place. The surplus carbon dioxide in the atmosphere contributes greatly to global warming, as we shall explain later, so it is important to control and limit its emission.

Carbon dioxide is not the only carbon-based gas that pollutes as a result of energy being generated from fossil fuels. *Carbon Monoxide* is also created by imperfectly burning fossil fuels. This occurs not only in power stations but also in central heating and hot water boilers, coal fires and car exhausts. It is a lethal gas and is not recycled into oxygen by plants. If it is inhaled in significant quantities it kills. Households, not cars and not heavy industry, create 77% of our carbon monoxide pollution.

Nitrogen Oxides are created when fossil fuels are burnt and some of the nitrogen in the air combines with oxygen. There is a range of chemicals involved but the most significant ones are nitrogen dioxide and nitrous oxide. High concentrations of nitrogen oxides damage health and they also harm plants. They also contribute to acid rain. Half of our production of nitrogen oxides comes from road transport with a further 20% from power stations. Burning coal creates twice the quantity of nitrogen oxides per unit of energy as oil, which in turn emits twice as much as gas. Although natural gas burns more cleanly, it still emits significant amounts.

The quantity of nitrogen oxides propelled into the air each year has been declining slowly but steadily since 1990, mainly due to catalytic converters on motor vehicles, and the reduction in the use of coal in generating electricity. It should not be thought, however, that the amount of these acid rain forming chemicals in the air is being significantly reduced; we are simply poisoning ourselves more slowly than before.

Burning natural gas does not produce sulphur emission but coal and oils frequently contain sulphur impurities, so that when they are burnt *Sulphur Dioxide* is produced in the form of an acid gas. Sulphur dioxide harms people and damages life and buildings when deposited as acid rain. By this we mean the various acidic gases, mainly sulphuric, which when emitted by combustion into the atmosphere, can be deposited either in rainfall – as wet acid rain, or in dust – as dry acid rain.

Some sulphur dioxide is emitted into the atmosphere naturally, particularly in volcanically active areas. At Smoking Hills, in the northern extremes of the Canadian Tundra, low grade coal at the surface sometimes spontaneously ignites causing sulphur clouds to be released. As the gas clouds move over the surface of the land the soil and freshwater become acidified. Local deposits of metals are dissolved which releases poisons into the air. Places like Smoking Hills are fortunately rare in nature. Most acid rain is produced as a result of man's unfortunate efforts.

Under certain conditions some dramatically noticeable pollution can take place, such as smog. One form of smog, known as industrial smog, is produced when sulphur dioxide and other pollutants are released by fossil fuel burning and are contained in a layer of cold air that is trapped by thermal inversion – a layer of warm air above it.

Smog can also be produced by nitrous oxides (usually due to the incomplete burning of petrol, a problem common to the internal combustion engines of all cars). This reacts with oxygen to form a complex mixture of pollutants – a photochemical smog, a noxious cocktail. Photochemical smog often combines with industrial smog to make an even richer, more lethal mixture.

Energy production is responsible for a massive 44% of the acid rain (produced by both sulphur oxides and nitrous oxides); manufacturing industry and agriculture together account for 26%, and private households for 11%. Clearly, by the widespread use of solar power as an energy source these emissions can be significantly reduced.

Pollution, in the various forms that we have described is an almost invariable consequence of our generating power and using it. However there are other harmful effects that are as insidious as atmospheric pollution and just as dangerous. One of the most dangerous is global warming.

Chapter 4

Energy and global warming

The theory of global warming is also called the Greenhouse Effect. It must be regarded as the most serious problem facing humanity today, more deadly and terrible in its effects than any known disease, human conflict or natural catastrophe. It is all the more frightening because it neither kills nor ravages like an epidemic, but strangles life out of the planet slowly but surely. It causes the very force that makes life possible on earth – the sun – to become the force that will ultimately destroy that life.

Everything originates with the sun, which until now has benefited our planet and created the conditions for life. The sun emits a huge amount of energy in the form of electromagnetic radiation, which has a very short wave-length. About 30% of the sun's radiation that reaches the earth is reflected straight back into space, because short wave radiation is harder for the atmosphere to absorb than long wave radiation. The remaining 70% penetrates the atmosphere. Some is retained there while the rest reaches and warms the surface of our planet and its waters. This warming drives the water cycle we are all familiar with – it causes water to evaporate and form clouds which then precipitate rain and snow.

Some of the radiation absorbed at the surface is reradiated in the form of long wave radiation which the atmosphere absorbs more easily than short wave.

Physicists have been pondering the Greenhouse Effect for far longer than most people would imagine. In December 1895 Svante Arrhenius presented a paper to the Royal Swedish Academy of Sciences about, as he termed it, "The Influence of Carbonic Acid in the Air upon the Temperature of the Ground". Apart from his own observations, which concentrated on what we would now call acid rain, Arrhenius drew on observations by the Irishman, Tyndall, in

1865, and the French scientist Fourier in 1827, to the effect that the atmosphere operates like "the glass in a hot house", trapping certain rays and letting through others.

Arrhenius concluded that increased amounts of carbon dioxide in the air made the atmosphere warmer. He believed that geological fluctuations in carbonic acids mainly from volcanoes, rock weathering and decomposition, were a cause of the Ice Ages. He blamed the increased amounts of carbonic acids that he was able to establish by his methodology in 1895 on coal production and use.

The modern theory of the Greenhouse Effect adds to these pioneering ideas. In addition to the trapping of heat by the atmosphere, greenhouse gases (mainly water vapour and carbon dioxide), also trap some of the outgoing energy before it can escape. As our way of life means that increasing amounts of carbon dioxide in particular are being emitted, the planet is warming up at a far greater rate than before, some would say at a dangerous and life-threatening rate.

Of course, there are many opinions about the degree of danger that we face from global warming. We should treat them with some caution and rely on those we perceive to be the most authoritative.

The United States Environmental Protection Agency, for example, believes that since the beginning of the Industrial Revolution carbon dioxide concentrations have increased by 30%, and those of nitrous oxides by 15% and those of methane more than doubled, and that these increases significantly enhance the ability of the earth's atmosphere to retain heat. They cite the following in support of their views:

The 10 warmest years of the 20th Century occurred between 1984 and 1999; 1998 was the warmest year.

Snow cover and floating arctic ice have decreased.

Global sea levels have risen by 10 to 25 centimetres over the past 100 years.

Precipitation over land has increased by 1% and the frequency of rainfall in the United States has also increased.

If the United States Environmental Protection Agency is right then there is indeed cause for grave concern. All commentators and scientists agree that water vapour and carbon dioxide trap heat in the atmosphere. If the temperature rises – even by, say, 1° Celsius over the next 100 years – the soil will become warmer and less moist, evaporation will increase causing more water vapour to exist in the atmosphere, and this will cause the atmosphere to retain more heat. It is as simple as that.

Are temperatures rising? Some observations over the past 100 years indicate a rise in that period of up to 1° Celsius. Global warming will cause rises in sea levels (mostly caused by the expansion of water as it becomes warmer with a tiny amount of help from melting ice caps). Warmer water can retain less oxygen than colder water and gives rise to more rainfall in higher latitudes and less at the equator. This is because precipitation is caused by warmer, moisture laden air meeting colder air; if the colder air moves further north so will the rainfall. This will cause deserts to expand further still; they are already expanding as a result of injudicious farming and forestry methods.

It is expected that apart from all the climatic change, there will be more violent rainstorms and drier soils with huge regional variations.

It should be pointed out that there is a great deal of division among informed scientific opinion about whether global warming is occurring and if so, whether its causes lie in the sheer volume of fossil fuels the world is now burning. Some scientists believe that the globe is not actually getting warmer. Sceptics argue that these are the scientists working for oil and coal businesses, but this is a disservice to an informed and honourable body of scientific opinion.

Accu-Weather, the leading commercial forecaster, reports that land based weather stations show an increase in temperature of about 0.45° Celsius over the past century. This, of course, may be no more than a normal climatic variation.

Weather satellite data appear to indicate a slight cooling of the climate over the past 20 years. The satellite data can be very confusing, especially the satellite measurements of the part of the earth's atmosphere which covers the area from the surface of the earth to a point some 10 to 15 kilometres high – the lower troposphere.

Some sources claim that 98% of the greenhouse gases are natural – mostly in the form of water vapour. Therefore, they argue, only 2% of the greenhouse gases are man-made – a tiny fraction of the amount involved. This seems to ignore the possibility that even a small amount of man-made greenhouse gas will marginally heat the globe causing more water vapour to be produced naturally.

Others say that the satellite data contain errors; when these are corrected, they will prove that the globe is getting hotter. This is vigorously denied by the fossil fuel industry. The argument centres on the accuracy of the instruments used to gauge the microwave radiation given out by oxygen molecules in the atmosphere, from which the air temperature can be calculated. Radiation levels are measured at a range of altitudes, including in the lower troposphere, so that the way the temperature measured is isolated is necessarily complex and the precise position is not certain.

The statistical complexities can be used by supporters of both sides, yet they are crucial both to the future of the multi billion pound fossil fuel business, and even more importantly to the future of our planet. Whatever the precise position may be, the vast majority of scientific opinion agrees that global warming is taking place.

Some scientists take the view that increased greenhouse gases are insignificant factors in global warming. Dr Sallie Baliunas of the Harvard-Smithsonian Center for Astrophysics believes that the real cause of global warming is the fluctuation that takes place in solar radiation. The sun does not emit its radiation at a steady rate but variably. Sunspots and unexplained phenomena can also vary the amount of heat radiated and thus affect the temperature of the planet. It is highly significant that best placed climate experts generally agree that global warming is taking place. They also point to the fact that glaciers in the Alps are melting, the sea level has risen by 10 to 25 cm over the past 100 years and sea corals are being bleached by high sea-surface temperatures. These factors are all consistent with an increase in global air temperatures.

Extensive studies of the United States climate show that night time temperatures have generally increased more than daytime temperatures. Extreme climatic events, such as tornadoes, hurricanes and storms have measurably increased in the United States, and it seems from our personal experience that these extreme events have also increased in the United Kingdom. In October 2000 parts of Bognor Regis, in Sussex, were devastated by two tornadoes occurring within days of each other. Heavy rainfall events in the U.S. have heightened in intensity.

Almost all specialists agree (the occasional exception may be made for experts employed by the oil companies) that without drastic steps to curb greenhouse gas emissions, the average global temperature will increase 1 to 3.5° Celsius during the next hundred years because effective levels of carbon dioxide are expected to double, probably within the next fifty years.

The human race is adapted to live within a very small temperature range. We cannot easily live at the poles or in the middle of a waterless desert. Even a change of 1° Celsius would greatly affect our way of life and probably the ability of many people to survive. During the so-called Little Ice Age, a period lasting from 1500 to 1850 when there were extensive glacial advances, the global temperature was only about 0.5° Celsius lower than it was in 1900. The Little Ice Age had a profound effect upon agriculture and was even responsible for migratory movements of humans leading to conflict and wars.

It is not surprising, therefore, that there is a general consensus amongst scientists that the higher temperatures projected for the next century will cause more frequent and intense heat waves, wide-scale ecological disruptions, a decline of agricultural production in the tropics and subtropics and the continued acceleration of sea-level rise.

One broad area of agreement is that levels of greenhouse gases in the atmosphere, primarily carbon dioxide, methane, nitrous oxide, ozone and hydrocarbons have grown significantly since pre-industrial times. During this period, the CO_2 level has risen 30% to more than 360 parts per million, methane 145% to more than 1,700 parts per billion and nitrous oxide 15% to more than 300 parts per billion.

The banning of CFCs helped to prevent the increase in one type of greenhouse gas, the carbon-hydro-fluorides, but in reality nothing has been done to prevent the continued increases of carbon dioxide in the atmosphere.

There has been a lot of speculation recently about whether more frequent hurricanes and more intense and longer lasting El Niño conditions are related to global warming. A warmer sea surface is the primary feature of global warming that might cause more significant hurricanes, but ocean circulation changes may counter the effects of this added warmth.

Since 1976, El Niño episodes have been stronger, more frequent, and more persistent than they were earlier in the century. Some of the models suggest that stronger, more frequent El Niño episodes would be a tendency in a warmer world. But there is no consensus in the scientific community about how these would change. Scientists are doing a lot of research to see if they can establish a cause-effect relationship between global warming and the change in the pattern of El Niño phenomena. In the western Caribbean off the coast of Belize, around the Cook Islands, and in the Philippines, massive coral bleaching has been observed since 1983. Coral reef bleaching results from the expulsion of symbiotic zooxanthellae algae from the coral reefs. The algae provide reefs with most of their colour, carbon, and ability to deposit limestone.

Raymond L. Hayes, Professor of Anatomy at Howard University, Washington, D.C., has studied the bleaching of corals. He found that coral bleaching occurs when the ocean temperature exceeds 30° Celsius for more than two weeks. The normal maximum ocean temperature in regions where corals live is around 28° to 29° Celsius. If the maximum temperature rises a modest one degree Celsius, reports Professor Hayes, the coral becomes bleached and cannot take in enough food or oxygen. If water temperatures return to normal the following year, coral reefs may recover, but if the coral is subjected to continued temperature rises, the reefs may die.

Another important indicator of a warmer planet is the retreat of alpine glaciers. In the tropics, every glacier appears to be retreating and the rate of retreat is accelerating. In Venezuela, for example, three glaciers have completely disappeared since 1972. In the temperate zones, most of the glaciers are also retreating.

Peru is particularly concerned about the accelerating melting of glaciers in the Cordera Blanca region of the Andes. The glaciers there provide Peru with irrigation water for its coastal desert and feed rivers that are dammed for hydroelectric power. Loss of glaciers would harm both power production and agriculture for the country.

It was thought that climatic changes in the past happened very slowly. However by measuring oxygen isotopes and dust in Greenland's ice cores and by studying glaciers in the Andes and in New Zealand's Alps, scientists have found that some of these temperature changes were very sudden, sometimes fluctuating 5 to 10° Celsius in less than twenty years.

Can the world adapt to global warming? If the climate does change can the world's natural ecosystems simply adapt to the changes with little adverse effect upon them? We doubt it.

Although we can point to the known climate changes that ecosystems have adapted to – the Ice Ages for example – we do not believe that the ecosystems can adapt satisfactorily in the sense of preserving the range of life that they now maintain.

The main reason is that the previous climate changes took place over thousands of years, whereas global warming is likely to cause significant climate change over the next ten or twenty years. Life can often adapt to very slow climate changes. There is no evidence of life being capable of adapting to climate change at the speed that global warming will bring about. It is theoretically possible that life will be capable of evolving and adapting, but natural history teaches that not all life will be capable of adapting and there is no assurance that human life will be able to adapt quickly enough to survive. One notable thinker, Professor Stephen Hawking, expects that humans can only adapt quickly enough to overcome its threatened extinction as a result of global warming if they can migrate to new worlds.

In addition, previous climate changes caused alterations in the natural environment. As the ice caps gradually retreated more suitable vegetation took root and animals slowly migrated or adapted. Today humankind has vastly altered the natural environment. Tropical rain forests have been cut down; temperate woodlands have been ploughed up. Pollution has also caused changes. These factors have probably made the ecosystems less robust and more dependent upon human management. They are now fragile and likely to be grossly affected by climate change.

Studies have shown that life on earth has always moved to favourable locations. Species of all life forms have been able to shift slowly into areas where they can prosper most. For example studies of plant fossils appear to indicate that plants can migrate to more favourable areas at rates of between 40 metres a year for the slowest and 2 kilometres a year for the fastest plants. However other studies indicate that temperatures could increase at a speed that require plants to migrate at rates of between 1.5 and 5 kilometres a year.

If plants cannot move as quickly as they need to, then individual plant species will die out and large volumes of vegetation will be lost. The globe's capacity for converting carbon dioxide into oxygen would be reduced. This could in itself contribute to further and even faster global warming.

Chapter 5

Energy and pollution from nuclear power

So far we have seen that atmospheric pollution and global warming are by-products of our use of energy. Nuclear processes, in power plants like the Magnox plants, generate a significant part of our electricity. Nuclear energy does not produce any carbon or sulphur gases as a by-product; it generates no blacksmoke. It does not contribute to global warming. It is marvellously clean except for one factor. It does produce as a by-product: radioactive waste.

Some sources have concerns that the nuclear industry is unsafe. We shall discuss this later. There may be accidents or accidental leakages of radioactive material. There is a debate as to whether there are significantly higher levels of leukaemia around nuclear reactors. Leaving aside these real concerns, there is one problem that must be addressed in every nuclear operation – that of what should be done with the radioactive by-product of used fuel.

Nuclear installations at Dounreay, Windscale (Sellafield), Harwell, Culham, and Winfrith are all being dismantled under the auspices of the Atomic Energy Authority. At Winfrith, in Dorset, the site opened in the mid-1950s and its main reactors were closed in 1991. Decommissioning is still going on and it is projected that the site will be safe enough to be used as a business park by 2025. That projection is likely to be overoptimistic.

The real problem is that there are only two basic options for used fuel – either direct disposal or reprocessing.

Before reprocessing, the potent used fuel must be stored for some five to ten years at reactor sites or reprocessing plants. During reprocessing, uranium and plutonium are separated and various intermediate- and high-level, wastes generated. Here we also find very long-lived, high-level, liquid waste. This is mainly the fission products and actinides other than uranium and plutonium.

Most potent of all used fuel is long-lived high-level solid waste.

The whole fuel assembly of the reactor is treated as waste. It is stored and cooled until its radioactivity and heat output have reduced enough to simplify handling, before it is made ready for packaging and final disposal. These storage and subsequent conditioning operations (called reprocessing) generate intermediate- and low-level waste.

There is also long-lived intermediate-level liquid waste, which arises from the various separation processes and which must be safely disposed of, together with intermediate-level solid waste, such as fuel claddings. In addition, there will be a variety of low-level wastes to dispose of.

Liquid high-level waste must be stored in cooled tanks for a number of years before being solidified by a vitrification process. Steel containers holding the vitrified waste are then stored, typically for 30 to 50 years, in air-cooled vaults. This is not the end of the process of making the high-level waste safe, but, sixty years after the waste was created, the process is merely beginning. The waste will be "geologically disposed of" by which the nuclear industry means that they will bury it in what they hope are stable rock formations for thousands of years. The nuclear industry will have evaluated the safety of the disposal site and the storage system, and they will assure us that their evaluation is 100% accurate. Without being over cynical, it seems to us that this long process must involve certain significant risks, no matter how much care is taken.

Low- and intermediate-level liquid waste are also created. These effluents (but not high-level waste) are sent to a waste treatment plant where they are stored in different tanks, depending on their nature. Two types of treatment can be used for decontamination: chemical precipitation or evaporation. The radioactive sludges, flocs, and evaporator concentrates that the nuclear processes create are solidified by being cast in cement, resins or bitumen.

Many people are rightly uneasy about the long-term storage and disposal of these dangerous by-products. Others feel strongly that the safety issues are not sufficiently addressed in the nuclear industry. The volume of highly radioactive irradiated or spent nuclear fuel has massively increased. Despite the huge scientific and economic input of a civil nuclear programme spanning forty years, there is still no accepted technique for disposing of the waste that inevitably results from the operation of nuclear reactors. There are now more than 130,000 tons of spent fuel from nuclear plants being stored in pools of water at reactors, and the amounts stored are increasing daily.

When things go wrong it is catastrophic. It is not too long ago that the accident at Chernobyl not only killed many people in the then Soviet Union but the release of radioactive material was measurable in livestock all over Europe. And yet we generated one third of our electric power from this source in 1997.

It is worth considering the damage caused by the events at Chernobyl in some detail because it will assist us in evaluating the real dangers of the nuclear industry.

On 26 April 1986, a nuclear reactor at the Chernobyl Nuclear Power Station, located 60 miles north of Kiev, in what was then the Soviet Union but is now the Ukraine, accidentally exploded. The accident occurred during an experiment designed to improve safety.

In all nuclear reactors a great deal of heat is created. Overheating is dangerous and so the power station engineers are constantly trying to find out whether they can improve safety and reduce the risk of overheating the nuclear core.

Chernobyl was designed to have its core cooled by water and its emergency core cooling system, designed and installed to prevent overheating, was powered by electricity. The power station engineers were rightly worried that if the electrical supplies to cooling pumps were to fail, the core might overheat. They had been conducting a series of experiments to discover the best way to prevent overheating.

On 26 April in the course of one of these experiments the engineers operated the nuclear reactor outside its normal range. They switched off the emergency core cooling system (for eleven hours) and operated the reactor at less than full power in order to establish whether the main pumps, powered by the residual electricity from a generator that was being slowly run down, would be able to cool the core.

When these types of power stations work at low output more steam than water gathers in the fuel tubes and consequently the number of neutrons available for the chain reaction actually increases. This flaw was overlooked at the design stage. Although they were reducing reactor power, the low flow of cooling water boiled, producing more steam, thus increasing the quantity of neutrons and causing the power to rise.

Eventually, as things started to go wrong, they shut down the generators. The cooling pumps powered by the generators slowed. This reduced water flow in the core, producing more steam. This caused the number of neutrons in the chain reaction to increase further and reactor power actually increased.

Two non-nuclear, but chemical, explosions occurred as a result of the interactions between steam and overheated fuel elements. The force of the explosions was equivalent to 200 tonnes of explosive. The reactor 'lid', (it weighed more than 2,000 tonnes) lifted off and tonnes of nuclear material escaped into the atmosphere.

The accident happened because of a combination of various factors – the power station was designed with fatal flaws, the operating instructions were ignored, and there was inadequate supervision of the power station staff.

At least 9 million people have been affected by the accident; 2.5 million in Belarus; 3.5 million in the Ukraine; and 3 million in Russia. Over 160 000 square kilometres of land was and remains contaminated. 400,000 people were forced to leave their homes. 270,000 people are living in places where they cannot eat food grown in their gardens or on their farms. Enormous economic losses were suffered and will continue to be suffered by Belarus, the Ukraine and Russia for many years to come.

In the UK the total cost of compensation paid to farmers exceeded £12 million and the government restricted normal activity on 219 farms with 317,400 sheep over an area of 1000 square kilometres. Several other European countries suffered even higher economic losses. In Germany, the Federal Government paid out 452 million DM (around £150 million), while in Austria, the government paid compensation for agricultural losses totalling 966 million Austrian schillings (around £50 million).

The human cost is greater. The Chernobyl accident has resulted in an increase of thyroid cancers in the three countries most affected. Already many cases of thyroid cancer have been recorded in Belarus, Russia and the Ukraine. Belarus has shown a hundred fold increase. Russia indicates a ten-fold increase and the Ukraine seven-fold.

UNICEF reports other significant increases in health disorders. Nervous system and sensory organ disorders have increased by 43%, digestive system problems by 28%; and disorders of bone, muscle and the connective tissues have increased by 62%. Malignant tumours have increased by 38%.

Some 800,000 people were employed immediately after the accident in fire-fighting and recovery work. Medical monitoring of some of them indicates growing morbidity and mortality rates. These heroes of the clean up operation have been rewarded with thyroid cancer (increased 4000%) diabetes (700%) diseases of blood organs (840%) and some malignant tumours (160%) and a general reduction in the functioning of the immune system.

These after-effects are devastating both in personal and global terms. In December 2000, after the rest of the world had made huge payments to persuade the Ukraine that it did not need its nuclear reactors at Chernobyl, all the remaining reactors at Chernobyl were finally closed down. A dozen of the same kind of Russian designed nuclear reactors remain in operation in the Ukraine.

The British Nuclear Industry claims that the kind of accident that happened at Chernobyl cannot occur in the UK. Our reactor designs do not have these design flaws. There is, they claim, better regulatory control with independent inspectors. They are right on those two specific points, but there have been lesser (but nonetheless serious) accidents and breaches of safety procedures at UK nuclear power plants. When humans attempt to harness nuclear energy safely they are playing with something much more dangerous than fire.

It has been estimated that, although different forms of radiation were released into the atmosphere, the total radioactivity from Chernobyl was 200 times that of the combined releases from the atomic bombs exploded at Hiroshima and Nagasaki. The real figures are not clear. Many of the official estimates at the time claimed that 50 million curies (excluding noble gases) were released. However, in 1995, the Committee on the Safety of Nuclear Installations from the Nuclear Energy Agency published the results of further research that indicated the release was actually three times greater than previously estimated.

As at 31 December 1995, there were some 430 commercial nuclear power reactors operating in the world with a collective nominal capacity of nearly 340 gigawatts (GW), producing about 17% of global electricity.

Seven years before Chernobyl there was an accident in another nuclear power plant. This time it was not poorly designed or inadequately regulated. It was operated in the most technologically sophisticated and power-greedy country in the world – the United States. The accident happened at a Pressurised Water Reactor at Three Mile Island nuclear power station near Harrisburg, Pennsylvania. The reactor was a new one and it overheated (or in the words of the nuclear industry "suffered a loss of cooling at the reactor core"), which resulted in partial melting of the core.

To avoid failure of the containment building, the fission product gases were released into the atmosphere 48 hours after the accident, and the hydrogen over a period of a few days. The area around the plant was temporarily evacuated while this was done. No general evacuation was carried out but it remained a possibility for several days. The accident caused no injuries and many highly regarded epidemiological studies conducted between 1981 and 1991 have found no measurable health effects to the population in the vicinity of the station.

Today, the Three Mile Island reactor is permanently shut down, with the reactor coolant system decontaminated, the radioactive liquids treated, most components removed and the remainder of the site being monitored. The owner, General Public Utilities Nuclear Corporation, says it will keep the facility in long-term storage until the operating license for the Three Mile Island power station expires in 2014, at which time the whole plant will be decommissioned.

Closer to home there have been scares and problems with nuclear safety at power stations in the United Kingdom. In October 1957 a fire occurred at Windscale in a military reactor used to produce plutonium for Britain's nuclear weapons programme. Overheating caused it and, as a result, releases of fission and activation products into the atmosphere occurred. The fire was eventually put out on Friday 11 October 1957 by simply flooding the reactor with water. There were tiny, but measurable, increased cancer risks – particularly thyroid and lung cancers. Compared with Chernobyl the release of dangerous material was tiny. Later the authorities renamed Windscale Sellafield.

The additional risks from the Windscale fire are small in comparison with normal cancer rates. Taking into account all measurements, the total fatal cancer risk from the Windscale fire to the most exposed individual is only marginally higher than the normal fatal cancer risk for a member of the UK population, according to the nuclear industry.

For many years now there has been a steady decline in the fortunes of the nuclear industry. We have seen the cancellation of nuclear power programmes and reactors around the world. Today, in Western Europe only France has any reactors under construction, while in Central and Eastern Europe only a handful of reactors are being built. In Asia reactor programmes are being slimmed down and cancelled. After a review of the privatisation of the British nuclear power industry, it was concluded that there was no economic justification for public funding to build any new reactors. In December 1995, Britain announced the cancellation of its two proposed nuclear power stations. In the next decade this downward trend is likely to continue, and as the true economic and environmental costs of decommissioning and radioactive waste management are discovered it could even accelerate more rapidly.

Some take the view that the nuclear industry has had almost 50 years to prove that nuclear technology is safe, clean and cheap and has failed to do so. It boasted originally that it would produce electricity "too cheap to meter" but now it is clear that the environmental and economic costs of nuclear power may well be too expensive to afford. Renewable energy sources have clear environmental and economic advantages over nuclear power.

Chapter 6

Energy and pollution from hydro electric projects

Hydroelectric power is generated by water flowing through turbines. Great falls are needed to make the generation effective and often vast volumes of water are needed to make the production of electricity commercially viable. When hydroelectric power is generated there is no atmospheric pollution, no radioactive waste and certainly this form of power can be pollution-free, or so it may be thought.

The problem lies with the large volumes of water that must be used. Many places are too flat to make hydroelectric generation effective. In some countries the rain falls in the wrong places and so large areas of water have to be collected and dams built for this power to be generated, and therein lies the difficulty.

Flooding large areas of land has environmentally damaging effects. First, there is the obvious loss of wildlife, vegetation and people's homes. Second, and less obviously, some scientists calculate that the decomposition of vegetation caused by flooded lands in dam projects gives off substantial amounts of carbon dioxide that, of course, contribute greatly to acid rain and to global warming.

Canada is a country that acquires more of its power from hydro-electricity than any other source. Canada has plans to flood large areas of land in Quebec to create dams for hydroelectric generating plants. It has already flooded over 10,000 square kilometres of land in the La Grande project in the James Bay region of Quebec and if further plans are carried out then the eventual area of man-made lakes caused by flooding in Northern Quebec will be an area that is larger than Switzerland.

It is feared that by flooding such a vast tract of land not only will greenhouse gases be created (which will be equivalent to those produced by burning fossil fuel) but there will also be a loss of rare ecosystems, flora and fauna. In other places, large dams have in addition destroyed the homes, communities and ways of life of peoples who have been indigenous in these areas for thousands of years. These are the hidden ill-effects of hydroelectric power.

Of course, hydroelectric power, which does not require flooding – where the turbines can be driven by the run of water without dams or reservoirs – would not be a source of greenhouse gases nor the other ill-effects described.

We should also mention the short-term problems of hydroelectric power. Damming a river can alter the amount and quality of the water in the river down stream and can prevent fish from travelling upstream to spawn. This can be (partially) resolved by fish ladders – but there is a limit to how high fish can climb. In addition, silt, normally carried downstream naturally by the flow of the river to where it fertilises the estuary lands, is no longer carried down to the river mouth where a dam intervenes. It slowly accumulates in the reservoir until it eventually decreases the amount of water that can be stored. For example, after only four years of being in full operation, the Sanmen Gorge dam, on the Yellow River in China, had lost over 40% of its water storage capacity and 75% of its 1,000 MW power capacity, due to the sediment build up in the reservoir.

Rotting vegetation under water becomes a rich habitat for bacteria. Bacteria can change the character of mercury, present in rocks under the reservoir, making the it water-soluble. Mercury then accumulates in the bodies of fish and, of course, it is dangerous to eat fish with mercury in their bodies. In the La Grande dam project mercury has been found in both the fish and the water.

The bacteria also change the quality of the reservoir water. New forms of bacteria can develop in these man-made lakes that can pose serious health hazards.

Finally, all large bodies of water, whether man-made or not, do influence the climate of the locality surrounding them. Water from reservoirs evaporates and as a result, humidity levels tend to be higher, causing more fog than normal. In tropical areas man-made lakes are thought to disrupt the convection cycle and ultimately reduce cloud cover.

There are some famous hydroelectric projects which, when they were conceived, were thought to have no significant polluting consequences but, as always, time presents the bill that must be paid.

Egypt built a 360 foot dam across the River Nile near Aswan. It is nearly two and a half miles long and stores one and a half billion cubic feet of water. It produces electricity and has helped control the flooding of the Nile, but has uprooted large numbers of the indigenous population and submerged ancient monuments. On the River Paraná between Paraguay and Brazil the Ituaipu Binacional power station feeds off an even bigger dam – nearly twice the size of Aswan. Turkey, a growing and thriving country, needs electricity and energy and has turned to hydroelectric power. Seven multinationals and eight governments, including that of the United Kingdom, are planning to build the Ilisu dam in south-east Turkey. The dam will displace 25,000 people from their homes and many farmlands (and accordingly livelihoods) will be lost. The dam will flood the medieval town of Hasankeyf where artefacts pre-dating biblical times are thought to exist. Clearly the environmental damage will be enormous. Critics point out that the affected persons are all Kurds and that, when considered with other existing dams, the flow of the ancient River Tigris will be controlled by Turkey, to the detriment of Iraq and Syria. If the dam proceeds, the United Kingdom intends to underwrite £200 million of the project.

One huge dam project in the course of construction is in China on the River Yangtze. China has conceded that the project is likely to cause serious environmental damage. The project will raise the water level by up to 250 feet over a 200 mile stretch of the river and will create a reservoir of 252 square miles. So far more than 100,000 people have been moved from small farms and towns close to the river. By 2003 another half a million people will have to be moved and another half a million three years later. China plans to rebuild villages and towns wherever possible further up the hillside. Critics argue that the higher slopes are mostly barren and the area is too isolated for businesses to be established there.

Like all major projects there are arguments for and against. The dam will help prevent flooding downstream and this is of extreme importance to the millions who live there. It will generate abundant electric power for central China, supplying more than ten large cities with electricity. However, most of the flooding downstream appears to be caused by tributaries rather than the Yangtze itself, and there will at the end of the project be more than one million people who have been forced to leave their homes.

Fifty or sixty years ago the United States considered that dams were mainly beneficial. After all, the Hoover Dam made the City of Las Vegas possible. Today there is a lobby for returning rivers to their natural ways. Policymakers are seriously considering pulling down hundreds of dams in states such as Wisconsin and Pennsylvania. Between 1990 and 1998 more than 200 dams were dismantled.

The reason behind this is environmental. Dams in many cases no longer serve much purpose and do a lot of harm by altering the natural flow of rivers and affecting the fish and other species that depend on them. There are about 75,000 dams in the United States, but only a few thousand are likely candidates for removal in the near future. Demolishing even a dozen medium-sized dams could consume billions of dollars and decades of effort, and come at a huge cost to the environment because of the enormous amounts of silt and sediment trapped behind the structures. Engineers and ecologists agree that dismantling dams, particularly the big ones that impound water in reservoirs, is a delicate and difficult operation. The silt and stones trapped behind the structures can clog the ecosystem downstream. In many cases, if the sediment were allowed to flush past the dismantled dams, it might smother the rivers, wiping out the very habitat the dam removals were undertaken to protect.

Chapter 7

United Nations efforts

Global warming, acid rain and pollution concern the world community. Many regard these issues as the most important that humanity faces today. It therefore comes as no surprise to learn that many worldwide organisations are sufficiently concerned to try to influence people's behaviour. However, as no worldwide organisation can at the moment achieve sufficient consensus to make binding and enforceable laws, they have to resort to issuing Declarations.

Many of these Declarations are no more than statements of hope and good intentions or best practice that are made while the makers of those statements continue in their wasteful ways. For example, the United States of America is the largest and most polluting of all countries in the world, and pollutes by itself more than several continents combined. Its insatiable appetite for energy causes it to produce one quarter of all pollution in the world for the benefit of its inhabitants who constitute only 4% of the world's population. If you add the pollution caused by the energy that goes into products consumed in the United States, the overall emissions created by or on behalf of the United States may well constitute one third of the World's pollution. The US government, through its various agencies, sagely warns about acid rain and global warming, yet while doing this they continue a system which allows wasteful burning of fossil fuel and the production of a bountiful supply of over-polluting motor vehicles at cheap prices.

The United States is not the only country to exhibit this hypocrisy. Sadly, it exists in every country in the world. There must be more statements of good intentions about environmental issues than any other topic.

The United Nations' environmental activities (when you exclude efforts to prevent the proliferation of nuclear weapons) first began in Sweden with the *Draft Declaration on the Human Environment* that was made by The United Nations Conference on the Human Environment, which met at Stockholm in June 1972.

It was a forward-looking declaration at the time motivated by "the need for a common outlook and for common principles to inspire and guide the peoples of the world in the preservation and enhancement of the human environment" as they rightly declared.

The Stockholm Conference proclaimed that both natural and man-made aspects are essential to well-being and to the enjoyment of basic human rights. It declared that the protection and improvement of the environment are major issues that affect the well-being of people and economic development throughout the world.

Having praised the resourcefulness and inventiveness of humankind it continued,

"We see around us growing evidence of man-made harm in many regions of the earth: dangerous levels of pollution in water, air, earth and living beings; major and undesirable disturbances to the ecological balance of the biosphere; destruction and depletion of irreplaceable resources; and gross deficiencies harmful to the physical, mental and social health of man, in the man-made environment, particularly in the living and working environment."

It argued that in the developing countries most of the environmental problems are caused by underdevelopment.

"Millions continue to live far below the minimum levels required for a decent human existence, deprived of adequate food and clothing, shelter and education, health and sanitation."

It pointed out that in developed countries environmental problems are generally related to industrialization and technological development. And then, in resounding language said,

"A point has been reached in history when we must shape our actions throughout the world with a more prudent care for their environmental consequences. Through ignorance or indifference we can do massive and irreversible harm to the earthly environment on which our life and well-being depend. Conversely, through fuller knowledge and wiser action, we can achieve for our posterity and ourselves a better life in an environment more in keeping with human needs and hopes. There are broad vistas

for the enhancement of environmental quality and the creation of a good life. What is needed is an enthusiastic but calm state of mind and intense but orderly work. For the purpose of attaining freedom in the world of nature, man must use knowledge to build, in collaboration with nature, a better environment. To defend and improve the human environment for present and future generations has become an imperative goal for mankind – a goal to be pursued together with, and in harmony with, the established and fundamental goals of peace and of world-wide economic and social development."

The Stockholm delegates called upon the governments and peoples of the world to exert common efforts for the preservation and improvement of the human environment, for the benefit of all people and for posterity.

The Stockholm delegates formulated 16 principles that they believed important. This was the beginning of what has been an elusive attempt to state environmental principles. Although there have been many initiatives, all of them muddle other rights and issues with specific environmental ones. Accordingly, no statement by any government or organisation about environmental matters has the clarity of such key documents in the world's history as the Declaration of Independence.

The Stockholm Principles include a *"fundamental right to freedom, equality and adequate conditions of life, in an environment of a quality that permits a life of dignity and well-being"* and a requirement that the natural resources of the earth and samples of natural ecosystems should be safeguarded for the benefit of present and future generations. Vital renewable resources must be maintained. Wildlife and its habitat have to be conserved. The earth's non-renewable resources must not be exhausted.

We see the first signs of UN concern about global warming in principle 6:

"The discharge of toxic substances or of other substances and the release of heat, in such quantities or concentrations as to exceed the capacity of the environment to render them harmless, must be halted in order to ensure that serious or irreversible damage is not inflicted upon ecosystems."

States were called upon to avoid damage to the seas and resources were to be made available to preserve and improve the environment.

States were urged to adopt an integrated and coordinated approach to their development planning *"so as to ensure that development is compatible with the need to protect and improve the human environment for the benefit of their population".*

Stockholm 1972 represented a first step by the international community towards coming to grips with environmental issues. As with many of these international attempts to resolve these issues Stockholm managed to incorporate into its Principles other statements about the evils of colonialism and apartheid. These institutions, albeit wicked and evil, were no more or less responsible for environmental damage than, say, capitalism, slavery, socialism or democracy. In our view to mix other issues into what should be clear environmental statements weakens the impact of all issues, and makes environmentalists appear emotive and irrational. What should be a clear position on, say, pollution, becomes muddied and muddled.

The United Nations sought to extract and proclaim what they hold to be the key principles of development of resources. In June 1992, having met at Rio de Janeiro and debated the issues of how nations should develop their own resources, the United Nations proclaimed 27 Principles that became known as the Rio Declaration on Environment and Development. In our view the key principles are:

> Principle 2: States have..."*the right to exploit their own resources...and the responsibility to ensure that (their) activities do not cause damage to the environment of other states".*

> Principle 4: *"environmental protection shall constitute an integral part of the development process".*

> Principle 8: *"States should reduce and eliminate unsustainable patterns of production and consumption".*

Many of the remaining 24 principles, while encompassing important and uncontroversial points do not really state principles that govern the exploitation of the environment, but rather make obvious statements of fact which simply serve to detract from the most important point of all – that environmental damage knows no political borders and that it is essential to prevent polluting and damaging activities. If we poison our planet we have no future. Rio does not go far enough.

Like many such declarations Rio embodies a series of statements that have been thrashed out as acceptable to the member states, rather than genuine principles from which we can understand how we should manage the environment. Generally, the United Nations member states placed greater importance upon their own sovereignty than upon the prevention of pollution and the protection of the environment.

Unfortunately the Rio Declaration is worded in uninspiring language that has failed to concentrate on the key issue of the control of pollution. The states attending Rio adopted "Agenda 21" in order to flesh out the bones of the principles. Here, they went some way towards addressing the problems.

Agenda 21 contains many important agreements where the states assented to diverse environmental measures ranging from managing fragile ecosystems, conserving biological diversity, combating deforestation and environmentally sound management of hazardous wastes, to issues that more closely concern the scope of this work – the protection of the atmosphere.

It is outside the scope of this work to discuss more than a small part of Agenda 21 but we must mention Section 28. Clearly, many of the problems of pollution and the solutions being addressed by Agenda 21 have their roots in local activities. Accordingly, the authors of Agenda 21 declared that the participation and cooperation of local authorities will be critical to its success. They rightly understood that local authorities construct, operate and maintain environmental infrastructures, oversee planning processes, establish local environmental policies and regulations, and assist in implementing environmental policies. They play a vital role in educating, mobilizing and responding to the public, in order to promote sustainable development.

In Section 28 the United Nations mandated all local authorities throughout the world to the following tasks:

By 1996 to undertake a consultative process with their populations and achieve a consensus on "a local Agenda 21" for the community;

To implement and monitor programmes which aim at ensuring that women and youth are represented in decision-making, planning and implementation processes;

To enter into a dialogue with their citizens, local organizations and private enterprises and adopt "a local Agenda 21". The process of consultation would increase household awareness of sustainable development issues;

To assess and modify local authority programmes, policies, laws and regulations to achieve Agenda 21 objectives.

To develop and employ, as appropriate, strategies for use in supporting proposals for local, national, regional and international funding.

Governments were charged with requiring local authorities to meet these objectives. The United Kingdom signed up to Agenda 21, committing all its local authorities to their appointed tasks. Has your local authority undertaken any of these tasks? You should ask them to inform you of what they have done, in practical terms, to fulfil their Agenda 21 responsibilities. No doubt they will have held a number of meetings, but pollution and global warming require practical solutions, not more hot air.

In our opinion local authorities could do much, for example, in the discharge of their planning functions and supervision of building regulations, to ensure new buildings incorporate some energy saving systems. They already prescribe rules about the levels of insulation in new houses. Why not also set regulations requiring new buildings – whether domestic or commercial – to have solar collectors? Incorporating these devices into the buildings at the design stage brings down costs significantly. We know of one case of a local authority who refused permission for solar collectors to be installed on the grounds that the collectors would not work!

Unfortunately, the wording of Section 28 is not sufficiently mandatory, and there is no real mechanism for incorporating detailed rules that follow logically from Agenda 21 into United Kingdom law, short of government legislation. At this stage such legislation seems remote. Even if they were incorporated beyond general statements there is little local authorities can do without being given the money to do it, and there is little sign of that happening at present.

The Nairobi Declaration is another important document. Ministers and others similarly charged with the duty of protecting their countries' environments drafted it in 1997. It defined the role of the United Nations Environmental Programme and strengthened it by enlarging the Programme's mandate to six key areas of environmental policy and action:

- to analyse global trends and provide policy advice and early warning of threats, promoting the best scientific capabilities;

- to develop international environmental law;

- to implement international norms and policies, and foster compliance and cooperative responses to environmental challenges;

- to strengthen its role in the UN and the Global Environment Facility;

- to facilitate cooperation and serve as a link between all players in the international environmental field;

- to provide advice to governments and institutions.

This mandate represents an advance on Rio, but a regression from what could have resulted from Stockholm. It is also a shame that UN members have not been able to give a mandate to the UN for effective policing. Without proper international policing much of what the UN decides will be ignored or abused.

At the end of May, in the year 2000, ministers with environmental responsibility and other heads of delegation met in Malmö, Sweden to review important and emerging environmental issues, and to chart a course for the future. They were deeply concerned that, despite what they wrongly (in our view) described as the many successful and continuing efforts of the international community since the Stockholm Conference, the environment and the natural resource base that supports life on Earth continue to deteriorate at an alarming rate.

They declared what they described as the major environmental challenges of the twenty-first century. We do not set out all of the described challenges because – of necessity – some of them involve formulations of words that were inserted presumably for political purposes. The important challenges according to the Malmö Conference are:

1. The growing trends of environmental degradation that threaten the sustainability of the planet must be arrested and reversed.

2. Not enough is being done; immediate employment of domestic and international resources, including development assistance, far beyond current levels is vital.

3. A framework of international environmental law must be evolved and national law developed as a basis for addressing environ-

mental threats we must all adhere to the precautionary approach.

4. The richest countries are consuming far too much of our resources. Care for the environment is lagging behind economic and social development, and a rapidly growing population is placing increased pressures on the environment.

5. Environmental problems arise from urbanization, climate change, the freshwater crisis, the unsustainable exploitation and depletion of resources, drought and desertification, and uncontrolled deforestation, thus increasing environmental emergencies and the risk to health and the environment from hazardous chemicals and pollution. These are all issues that need to be addressed.

6. Technological innovations and the emergence of new resource-efficient technologies provide a source of hope and increased opportunities to avoid the environmentally destructive practices of the past. The private sector has an essential part to play in this.

7. Environmental considerations must be part of decision-making.

8. The environmental perspective must be taken into account in economic policy-making at government level and in the decisions of multilateral lending and export credit agencies.

Somewhat naively, in our view, Malmö described the private sector as having "emerged as a global actor that has a significant impact on environmental trends through its investment and technology decisions".

Of course, the private sector has always been critically important and central to initiating environmental trends. It has most often been more important than governments. For example, it is the private sector that, by marketing, creates demand, such as for hardwood from the tropical rainforests or for cars, by designing and marketing cheap and affordable models. States never founded oil exploration companies and coal mining ventures when they were highly speculative, although they may have nationalised them after they were established and successful, or strategic businesses.

Generally, the private sector acts without regard to the long-term view. In a world economy where joint stock companies' shares can change hands in a moment, the owners of, say, oil companies are a fluid and potentially changing corpus. There is no logic in their directors taking a long-term view. Furthermore there is an element of unaccountability in multinational corporations whose annual profits may be more than the gross national product of a medium-sized country and who employ tens of thousands of people in key sectors.

The private sector has always been responsible for much of the pollution and the environmental damage that flows from it. As consumers we cannot blame the corporations. After all, we buy the cars they produce and consume the electricity they generate.

What is true, however, is that the private sector can be harnessed to redress environmental wrongs. If the government can create a business environment where companies can make a profit from providing solar collectors that reduce emissions and pollution, then the profit motive will ensure their wide distribution. If the government can ensure that those products in which an individual has to invest are provided with a tax incentive, then people will vote with their wallets. In many situations, however, environmentally conscious consumers do the sums and find that although installation works in the long-term, there is simply not enough incentive in the short- to medium-term.

In this regard, governments have a crucial role in creating an enabling environment. As the Malmö conference proclaimed *"The institutional and regulatory capacities of governments to interact with the private sector should be enhanced"*.

Certainly, companies in the private sector that are responsible for pollution should be made accountable through the application of the "polluter pays" principle, environmental performance indicators and reporting, and the establishment of a precautionary approach in investment and technology decisions. In our view, although these are important, it is equally important to create an environment in which the person cleaning up pollution profits, as well as making the polluter pay.

The "polluter pays" principle is important, but we wonder how often the polluter really does pay more than a token towards the real cost of environmental damage. What compensation does a person receive for a spoiled view? Mining operations dirtied much of the Durham coastline, rendering it bleak and useless for amenity purposes. Although it has been largely cleaned up, no resident received compensation for being unable to enjoy the beach, or swim in the sea. What compensation does the asthma sufferer receive from motorcar users? What compensation does the real sufferer from pollution receive for his or her distress?

If we set up a system of rules that business interests can use in order to make profits, and in the course of their activities they pollute, why should their liability for pollution be limited to the cost of clean-up operations? The polluter at best pays for some clean-up, but never, ever, the whole cost, and never enough to reinstate the environment in the condition it was before it became polluted .

Chapter 8

European Community efforts

Closer to home, the Council of Europe has resolved that by 2010 Europe should be producing 12% of its energy from renewable sources. It has established a "Campaign for Take-Off" to achieve this end. The Campaign funds and encourages pilot schemes for renewable energy projects.

The Campaign for Take Off has identified certain specific key sectors which are to be promoted, and a number of ambitious targets:

One million Photovoltaic Systems; these high-technology systems generate electricity from solar energy. They involve roof top cells. It is, in our view, a relatively immature technology, although some improvements are made every few years. The sunshine requirement makes them suitable for southern Europe, rather than temperate climates, although there are potential uses for public buildings, summerhouses in Scandinavia (where they can use the long daylight hours) and some rural household electrification.

15 million square metres of solar collectors; the Council of Europe describes thermal collector technology – the types marketed by Genersys – as "almost fully mature" and states that "high quality products are available, solar systems are reliable and their productivity can be guaranteed". Domestic hot water is the main application although there are also space-heating and air-conditioning applications. The Council does not distinguish between vacuum collectors and solar panels. It would be fair to ascribe, out of the overall Council of Europe target figure of 15 million square metres, some one million square metres to the United Kingdom at a rate of 100,000 square metres a year. By the beginning of 2001, one company had installed only 6,000 square metres of collectors in England alone. We doubt that all the other companies combined installed more than another 10,000 square metres, so as a country we are falling well short of our target.

10 MW of wind turbine generators: wind energy represents what the Council regards as one quarter of all the potential renewable energy sources that can be utilised. The technology works but smaller, lightweight and more flexible designs and more reliable turbines are needed to bring this renewable resource to the optimum.

10,000 MW of combined heat and power biomass installations: biomass comprises residues of the woodworking industry, energy crops such as wood, peat and agricultural residue and the organic part of urban waste. Although this is renewable and to an extent involves recycling, it is not free of by-products in the same way as wind and solar power are and many of the advantages of other renewable sources are not present.

10 Million Dwellings heated by biomass: 85% of all EC housing is heated by single house systems. The number of houses that are heated traditionally by wood furnaces is declining. With modern efficient wood furnaces emissions drop dramatically and efficiency improves from 55% to around 90%. In Austria, Denmark and Finland, wood furnaces are used to heat whole districts and communities. The cost of investing in efficient wood burning power stations is very high.

1,000 MW of biogas installations: in this case the Council hopes to harness the methane gas produced in landfill sites and by livestock. Small experimental operations are in place and, although we hope that we are wrong, the Council's projection of 15% energy derivation from this source by 2010 looks somewhat optimistic.

5 Million tonnes of liquid biofuels: these, such as oil from rapeseed, compete directly with the oil industry and have the advantage of being renewable annually but there are other disadvantages.

Development of energy self-reliance in 1000 communities.

The overall investment in the Campaign for Take Off will cost, it is estimated, 30 billion euros, but of this less than one quarter will come from public funds. The Council itself will contribute less than one billion Euros, the remaining six billion coming from the tax-payers of national governments.

In cities and towns, apartment blocks and office blocks can be converted to using some form of renewable energy, probably solar. In rural villages and provinces, solar energy will be more viable if energy self-sufficiency is sought, because solar input can sometimes be larger than the energy consumed. Certainly, isolated farms and small villages could easily become virtually self-sufficient in energy if they used a combination of solar collectors to heat water and space, and wind turbines to generate current.

Although anything that reduces our dependence on fossil fuels is to be welcomed, it seems to us that the thrust of the European Commission's policy is wrong. Rather than achieve the 12% use of renewables by developing energy self-reliance in given communities, we think that it would be better to aim for greater use of genuinely free forms of energy within our existing frameworks. Trying to achieve complete energy self-reliance may be like trying to discover the secret of perpetual motion, but careful use of solar collectors and wind turbines will generate energy and power from sources which will not deplete their basic reserves – the sun and the wind – as they provide energy.

The Campaign for Take-Off suggests that wind and solar energy are the key sources. The Campaign recognises specifically that solar thermal collectors for domestic heating require investment by house-holds in renewable energy supplies. How can we encourage house-holds to invest in solar collectors?

Ideally, in the United Kingdom, Council Tax could be used to encourage the installation of solar collectors. A modest discount – say 10% - off the Council Tax payable once a system has been installed would encourage installation and improve the financial incentives. It is important to create these incentives. Fuel prices are transient, as we shall see, but a permanent saving attached to a dwelling does have appeal for most taxpayers.

As for businesses, the United Kingdom Government has set up a tax regime that positively discriminates against the deployment of solar collectors. We shall discuss this in Chapter 9.

In the same way that many consumers change from gas to oil or from oil to gas as the cost of one fuel increases in relation to the other, so in our view the assurance of permanent fiscal advantage would increase the take-up in solar. Then it will really "take off".

In fairness to the Council of Europe, it does state that there will be a directive to promote renewable energy sources and to provide tax reductions for renewables. But while we wait for the directive and more critically its implementation, fossil fuels burn.

We have set out the existing sources of our energy and the likely additional sources of the not too distant future. Wherever it comes from, energy makes our lives healthier, more convenient, safer, less risky, more comfortable and more luxurious. We can bath in hot water as often as we want to, we can eat exotic food from distant places, kept in a fit condition by energy that freezes or cools it, we can be hugely entertained with television, radio and music. Many forms of music these days can only be performed with a ready supply of electricity. If we are ill, hospitals can store blood for transfusions, give us antibiotics, and keep us alive even while operating on our vital organs, but only with the use of energy.

But for all these advantages, there are other aspects of energy consumption – the disadvantages of what happens when we create, transmit, and use it, and the potentially devastating effect that this has upon our planet.

We have seen how the United Nations Organisation and the European Community are endeavouring to encourage the use of more "green" power. The environmental advantages are apparent to all, but some people recognise that "green" power is not merely advantageous, it is critical to the welfare of all life on our planet.

Chapter 9

United Kingdom efforts

The United Kingdom is a member of the United Nations and an important constituent part of the European Union. All European Union countries are obliged by treaty to follow the initiatives that we have examined. However, in addition to these treaty obligations, the United Kingdom has been examining what else should be done. The Government has specifically decided to promote energy efficiency as a desirable goal.

It cites three main reasons for promoting energy efficiency. The first is the economic reason. The Government recognises that the costs of becoming energy efficient may in certain cases – they point to rented property – be uneconomic. Some households simply do not have the capital sums to lay out in order to make energy savings and are doomed to having to pay for expensive, inefficient energy.

The second reason the Government believes it is important to promote energy efficiency is a social reason. Clearly, people on low incomes and people of limited means are particularly helped by energy efficiency because they can live warmer, more comfortable lives. For these people, energy efficiency means cheaper energy.

The third is the environmental reason. Most carbon dioxide emissions in the United Kingdom are due to energy use and carbon dioxide is the main cause of the Greenhouse Effect responsible for climate change. The United Kingdom has a legally binding treaty obligation to reduce greenhouse gas emissions by 12.5% to 1990 levels by 2008-2012. The Government has set a separate non-binding target of reducing these emissions by 20% from 1990 levels by the year 2010.

Energy Efficiency Standards of Performance ("EESOPs" - also known as energy efficiency targets) are the means by which it is hoped to make energy use more efficient in the future. Since 1994

EESOP schemes, focusing on pensioners and low income groups, have led to more than 10 million compact fluorescent lights, 150,000 energy efficient appliances and 160,000 cavity wall insulations being installed in homes in our country. In February 2001 the Government announced that EESOP schemes would in future include solar energy provision; Genersys solar collectors qualify under this scheme.

A new EESOP, EESOP 4, will apply to gas distributors and electricity suppliers. This will, it is expected, require there to be energy efficiency savings for consumers but there will be no requirement upon the energy distributor to spend any sum of money. The distributors will be free to choose how they make savings, but Ministers have some input and will presumably continue to press for energy savings to be focused on pensioners and poorer people. Savings will be measured by lower consumer bills and lower consumption fairly apportioned between all the energy distributors, with the Industry Regulator playing a key role in approving and measuring whether the performance target is being met. As the gas and electricity suppliers can now install solar collectors as part of their energy efficiency strategy, they will, if they take up collectors, be easily able to meet the targets for energy efficiency.

Most of the EESOP program is directed towards traditional measures. In order to calculate the EESOP score certain assumptions have to be made on how long the installation will last. Accordingly, it will be assumed that cavity wall insulation lasts for 40 years, loft and internal wall insulation for 30 years, double-glazing, tank and pipe insulation for 20 years, thermostatically controlled radiator valves for 25 years but condensing boilers for only 15 years. These are all proven energy savings methods.

These are important measures, but they are indicative of just how unsatisfactory much of our housing infrastructure must be. Although the insulation and other measures are important, there are other ways to reduce greenhouse gases and reduce power plant energy consumption, for example by households being actively encouraged to install their own power plants in the form of solar collectors.

According to the Department of Industry, about 1% of our energy consumption is met from renewable resources. Their Energy Account shows some interesting figures and here in all cases we quote the 1997 figures. Then, the energy lost in the transformation and distribution of fuel was greater than the energy actually consumed in the home. After these losses in transformation and networking have been allocated to the end-user, domestic use of energy (including domestic car transport) is by far the largest, using the equivalent of 82,269,000 tonnes of oil – about the same as the amount used by industry and transport combined.

A central part of Government policy is the diversity of supply. It does not want to rely on any single fuel, technology or system for delivering fuel to the population. Therefore we must, it surmises, keep as many sources of energy as possible going, and use as many different systems of distribution as possible.

In this respect we think the Government is failing to perceive the benefits of a properly thought out solar power policy. By using solar collectors of the type that Genersys supplies, diversity and security of supply are enhanced. Individual homes and businesses will in effect be creating their own hot water, and, as the all-important expertise surrounding this technology improves, their own central heating. Individual households will be less dependent on any system of gas, oil or electricity distribution, although they will still have some significant requirements.

In these circumstances, it is of paramount importance that there should be positive benefits to those who have the foresight and concern to install solar collectors, and some financial incentive for not poisoning the environment. These people lay out large sums and ought to receive direct recognition and encouragement, including abolition of Value Added Tax on the purchase and installation of all solar collectors, fast track fee-free planning for the installations (where required), and specific permanent reductions in Council Tax on dwellings fitted with collectors.

Genersys has been lobbying the Government for a modest permanent Council Tax reduction for households who have had the foresight and sense of responsibility to install solar collectors. If the principle is agreed then a more appropriate, higher percentage discount should follow. On a long-term basis it makes sense to differentiate substantially between "green" and "dirty" households, subject to the over-riding importance of fuel poverty. In our view, a 35% Council Tax discount for "green" dwellings is justifiable on the grounds that the "polluter should pay" the cost to the country of the carbon dioxide emissions that a "dirty" or "non-green" household expels. Large grants can be made for the installation of collectors in low cost housing and in households suffering from fuel poverty.

As far as encouraging commerce and industry to use renewable energy sources is concerned, the Government has introduced a Climate Change Levy, which will take effect on businesses using energy from April 2001. It seems that the tax raised by the levy will be "recycled" by the Government back into business in a way that is intended to encourage energy efficiency, although we shall discuss the "recycling" aspect later.

The tax applies to natural gas, electricity, oil, coal and all similar fuels (except fuels used in road vehicles) which business, commerce and industry use for heat, light and power. It does not apply to non-business use of energy or energy used by charities. Additionally, public transport is exempt.

The tax is calculated by applying a rate to a theoretical nominal unit of energy. The Government, following the recommendations in an earlier report by Lord Marshall, decided that it is virtually impossible to relate the Climate Change Levy to the amounts of carbon dioxide emitted by each form of energy used. Using the energy content of fuels is thought to be simpler and would not encourage industry to switch from one fuel to another because of tax reasons. However, the Government, in adopting this approach, is not penalising the fuels that emit large amounts of carbon dioxide it considers because it considers that having diversity of fuel supply is more in the national interest than reducing global warming.

Furthermore, under these plans, all electricity is to be treated equally, whether generated by coal power stations or by renewable non-polluting wind farms.

The Levy is expected to raise about one and three quarter billion pounds in its first full year. That is about the same amount as the TV licence fee raises for the British Broadcasting Corporation. In real terms raising £1.75 billion from businesses that pollute in order to give it back to businesses seems a roundabout way of doing things. It seems to us that the Climate Change Levy could be a valuable tool in combating pollution and global warming, but in order to become useful it needs to develop so that it provides real encouragement for industry and commerce to install renewable sources of energy instead of using fossil fuels.

The formulae for calculating the Climate Change Levy vary according to the fuel used. It seems that a rough rule of thumb is to establish first whether the business pays Value Added Tax on fuel at the full rate – 17½%. If it does it is liable for Climate Change Levy.

We expect the levy to be equivalent (roughly) to a 10% surcharge on the electricity bill and a 15% surcharge on the gas bill. Customs and Excise will collect the levy and we explain the details below.

We doubt whether the majority of businesses paying Value Added Tax at the full rate really understand how the Climate Change Levy will increase their costs. In principle it should act as a real incentive for businesses to think about creating less carbon and using less fuel.

The Levy charge varies according to the fuel used. Gas purchased from a Utility incurs an additional tax of 0.15p per kilowatt-hour. The charge for electricity is 0.43p, for calor and propane type products 0.96p and for coal 1.17p. The price differentials are intended to create a level playing field between the various fuel types and do not in practice penalise any single fuel.

The measures that the Government has introduced to ensure that business is not adversely affected by the Levy include a 0·3% reduction in Employers' National Insurance Contributions, some standard exemptions (such as for very small business energy users) and special reductions for intensive energy users.

This is apparently to ensure that no loss of employment is caused by the Levy. It is beyond the scope of this work to comment on the Government's fiscal policy, but it seems to us that the "polluter pays" principle could be better adhered to if the Levy was used in a specifically environmental way – perhaps on the infrastructure spending that is becoming essential as a result of climate change, like improving sea defences, and providing an incentive for renewable energy use by everyone. As we have seen, it is not just business and industry that creates carbon dioxide. All of us do this and all of us should be encouraged to act in a more environmentally friendly way.

Certain business uses of energy – such as the energy used to propel trains – do not attract the levy, unless the energy is used to propel a train in a place of recreation – such as a theme park. Certain specific industries – cement, brewers, motor manufacturers, steel makers and renderers to name but a few – have special agreements and special discounts. If a business is covered by one of these special agreements it will need to "commit" to achieving the reductions specified by the agreement in order to benefit from the reduced Levy.

Overall, the need to apply for a specific reduction requires some complicated calculations (for example the energy used for in-store food preparation may be exempt but the energy used for lighting and heating the store is not exempt) and makes the Levy overcomplicated and overly bureaucratic. The exemptions detract from the "polluter pays" principle.

Of course, the Government is concerned about loss of competitiveness and does not want to penalise British Industry, which already competes with cheap or subsidised energy in other countries. The complexity of the Levy is a real problem. It confuses what should be a simple message.

A business pays tax on its profits. These are calculated by deducting from its earnings most expenses. Some costs are not deducted in the normal way. If a business invests in machinery that may last twenty years it is not usually possible to deduct the cost of the machinery in the year it buys it, but a slice of the cost must be deducted each year over the life of the machinery. Because the machinery expenditure is viewed as "capital" the deductions are called "capital allowances". As you will appreciate the above is a very simplified picture, but for the purposes of considering what happens in the United Kingdom when a business is thinking of investing in solar technology it can be taken as accurate.

In some parts of the country where the Government wanted to encourage businesses to establish themselves, it introduced a system of allowing all the capital expenditure to be written off against profits in one year. In order to encourage "green" energy the Government has a system of "Enhanced Capital Allowances" under which all costs of energy saving technology are written off in the year the costs are incurred; this accordingly represents a real tax saving for the business.

The problem with the scheme originally was that the Government stipulated that although *low*-carbon producing technologies like condenser boilers could qualify for enhanced capital allowances, *non*-carbon producing technologies like solar collectors could not qualify. If a large business produced low carbon emissions it could write off the costs of equipment that produces those carbon emissions, but if it used equipment that produces no carbon or other emissions it could not.

In February 2001, after intensive lobbying, the Department of the Environment and Regions confirmed that it would apply to the Inland Revenue for permission to include Genersys Solar Tubes as qualifying for Enhanced Capital Allowances. In the March budget in 2001 the Chancellor of the Exchequer announced that the solar technology employed by Genersys would qualify for Enhanced Capital Allowances.

Tax is an important tool that should be used to encourage laudable behaviour and in particular correct environmentally acceptable behaviour. By taxing unacceptable behaviour, governments can create real incentives and disincentives. For many years governments have not made use of the tax system to control anti-environmental behaviour. Slowly, however, they are changing their ways.

A combination of a high Climate Change Levy with fewer exemptions and special agreements combined with a system of tax incentives would cause businesses and individuals to adopt usable and mature technologies, such as solar energy, as a matter of course. Once industries – such as the brewing industry – use solar energy they will actually increase competitiveness because the solar energy is free after the initial capital costs have been repaid. Other important tools – changes in the planning laws and building regulations are also necessary, but the key instrument available to the Government is tax, and by overhauling the tax laws from an environmental viewpoint, renewable carbon-free energy will benefit us all.

Chapter 10

Energy use in the world

We have seen how energy is used in the United Kingdom, but of course, although the United Kingdom is a highly developed country, it is a small part of the world community. It consumes plenty of energy, but relatively less than the United States, where the climate conditions are more extreme.

There is a massive difference in the amount of energy a person in a developed country, like the United Kingdom, uses when compared with the energy used by a person in an undeveloped or developing country.

Let us first consider some of the facts; in 1970 the world, it is estimated, consumed 206 quadrillion British Thermal Units of energy. Two thirds of this was consumed by developed nations, with the United States being responsible for about 30% of world energy consumption. Today world consumption is probably around four hundred quadrillion, with the United States being responsible for about a quarter of that. Most predictions provide for the energy consumption growth of developed nations compounding at around 1% a year but for developing nations consumption is compounding at over 5% a year. If you do the mathematics you find that by 2015 the United States will be down to one fifth, but world consumption will have risen to over five hundred and sixty quadrillion.

Wherever energy is consumed, statistics show that consumption is on the increase and will continue to increase as undeveloped nations develop, and as developing nations reach developed status.

According to the Energy Information Association the *increase* in energy consumption in the twenty-year span from 1995 to 2015 will be equivalent to the total world energy consumption in 1970 – just before the oil crisis. Two thirds of this growth will, they predict, occur in developing countries and in countries whose economy is in transition. The growth energy use in developed countries, like the United Kingdom and the United States of America, is predicted to average around 1% a year, but growth in consumption by the developing nations of South East Asia in particular, will comfortably exceed 5 or even 6%.

Unfortunately, most of the growth will be as a result of increased fossil fuel consumption. Oil use is expected to exceed 100 million barrels a day by 2015 – which is a 50% increase in the oil used in 1995. More coal will be burnt and most of the increase will occur in India and China; their increased use of coal will vastly outweigh any further diminishing of coal use in Western Europe and North America. The use of natural gas is expected grow at over 3% a year, so that by 2015 its use will be equivalent to two thirds of the projected oil consumption for 2015. At the moment natural gas consumption is around 55% of oil consumption.

What is most striking about the Energy Information Association's predictions is their suggestion that only 8% of projected growth in energy demand over the next two decades will be served by non-fossil fuel sources. They believe that the non-fossil fuel share of world energy consumption will decline from 15% to 12% over the period to 2015.

If they are right, world carbon emissions are likely to increase by 3.7 billion metric tons, or 61%, over the 1990 level, by 2015. We have seen that the Climate Change Convention of 1992 requires those who have signed it to search for and develop policies to moderate or stabilize carbon emissions. However, even if all the developed countries were able to achieve stabilization of their emissions relative to 1990 levels, overall world carbon emissions would still rise by 2.5 billion metric tons over the next two decades.

Each individual living in one of the world's industrialised economies uses far more energy than an individual living in a newly emerging economy. This relationship is not expected to change significantly in the next two decades. In some emerging economies (for example, India and China), per capita energy use may double, but even with such growth, average per capita energy use in the developing countries will still be significantly less than one-fifth the average for the industrialized countries in 2015.

Clearly, the main factor that will drive this increase in consumption of energy is the natural desire among all nations to grow and improve their conditions. We should pause to consider the position of the average person living in developing countries.

More than four billion people live in developing countries. This is more than 80% of the world's population. Three billion of them live in countries where the gross national product is less than 350 dollars per person each year. These are very poor people. Their poverty is directly related to environmental degradation and this directly affects their health and ability to improve their living conditions by their own hard work. They suffer from contaminated water, poor, often poisonous, air quality inside their homes caused by wood, charcoal and dung burning for cooking and heating, and they suffer from high levels of outdoor air pollution caused by industries with which they have no connection or benefit. They also suffer from their forests being cropped and their farmland being degraded.

These inhabitants of developing countries are, on any basis, the people who make the least contribution to pollution and global warming. As we have seen, all major projections indicate that this will be the case for many years to come.

Their only hope for a better life is that their countries will develop industries, services and productivity that will provide better employment and safer living conditions together with stability and peace. In order to do this their countries must embrace a positive attitude towards development and use facilities, financial expertise and advice from the developed world. In addition, the developing countries know that they must provide energy for their people so that the businesses and industries can flourish and the people live decently and healthily.

In these circumstances it would not be surprising to find the developing countries adopting indiscriminate energy policies so that they can grow more quickly. Although this has been the case in the past many states in the developing world are re-thinking their energy policy. As a result government intervention in energy markets is becoming more influenced by concerns about global warming and the greenhouse gas implications of continued reliance on fossil fuels. Inproved policies towards local air pollution are also causing change.

The energy consumption of many developing nations is concentrated in a few major industries that are highly energy intensive and often use energy inefficiently. This results from using less proficient technology, having smaller factories and failing to maintain energy-efficient operations within them. These industries usually produce chemicals, primary metals, cement, and pulp and paper. They are all industries that are necessary for the development of infrastructure upon which economic growth is founded.

China is the world's largest consumer of coal. As a consequence, China's particulate and sulphur oxide pollution is among the most extreme in the world. Until recently Chinese policy has encouraged the use of its coal resources. Pollution control technologies used in the Western industrialised countries to reduce the environmental impact of coal use are not widely used in China.

China has primarily used cleaner burning coal that is available in the northern regions of the country and is transported by rail to the southeast regions where the bulk of the economic development is taking place. However, the rail system carrying the coal is running at full capacity so the coal is being stockpiled at the mines. Abundant reserves of coal are available much closer to the southeastern economic growth areas, but the product here is brown coal with lower energy content and a much higher level of pollutants. What should China do? Should it expand its capacity to transport the cleaner fuel from the north, build electricity generation capacity in the north and a transmission system to bring the electricity to the south, or should it use the more polluting coal that is closer to the places where it will be used?

Notwithstanding this heavy use of coal, China has a highly developed passive solar industry. Most of the solar collectors produced serve the home market, with only a fraction available for export, but those that are exported are, on the whole, well made and of very high quality.

It is important to understand what is happening in China because China has an energy intensity that is among the highest in the world. It is the most populous country in the world and it will inevitably be an important factor in the overall energy picture.

An interesting example of a developing nation that has suffered heavily from pollution caused by poor energy and environmental management is Mexico. In some parts of Mexico City – the world's largest city – the sewers are visible ten metres above the ground. It is one of the modern wonders of the world.

The sewers were laid below ground level in the1930s but Mexico City is sinking. So much water has been pumped out from the aquifer under the sewers to meet the needs of Mexico City's 18 million inhabitants that the land is sinking fast leaving behind the sewerage system firmly anchored in a hard layer of subsoil.

But Mexico is responding with more vigour and commitment to

the present situation than almost any developed nation. It has appointed an Environment Minister who has the equivalent of cabinet rank. He must be present when key cabinet discussions of any importance take place. He is not just an environmental figurehead but is a person who represents the environmental position in government; the importance that Mexico places on the need to frame all policies from an environmental viewpoint is shown by the rank the minister has been given.

It is a mistake to see environmental issues as somehow being "outside" the economy. This is an error common both to those who advocate giving environmental issues very low priority in the interests of economic development, and to those who see economic development as being necessarily bad for the environment. Mexico recognises that good environmental management requires decision-making processes which incorporate consideration of all those potentially affected by any proposed policy. This can only happen where all issues, particularly energy issues, are considered not only from an economic viewpoint but also an environmental viewpoint. In democracies such consideration can only arise if a senior member of the government is appointed specifically and given befitting authority.

Clearly, the industrialised countries, in particular the United States and the members of the European Community, need to take the lead in pollution reduction and energy efficiency. They must also change consumption patterns. China is rapidly becoming a success story of how poorer countries can tackle their emissions of greenhouse gases. China has cut its energy consumption per unit of output by half since 1980 during a period of rapid growth, whereas the United States could not commit to cutting its greenhouse emissions by 7%.

Another leading nation, India, is developing some critically important ideas about energy. Dr. R.K. Pachauri, Director of the Tata Energy Research Institute in New Delhi, believes that national security also involves the concept of environmental security. There are 2.8 billion people who live on less than $2 a day, and their environmental conditions and personal health are inexorably related to the lack of economic prosperity. Dr Pachauri feels that to attain environmental security a state must minimise environmental damage and promote sustainable development. Developing countries also usually lack the infrastructure and institutions to respond to crises, thereby increasing the likelihood of violent reactions.

Pachauri has identified five areas where poverty has either exacerbated or been exacerbated by natural resource stress. First, the need to provide food, shelter and clothing is increasing land degradation. Second, worsening pollution affects the quality of the air. Third, world climate change has led to a rise in both temperature and sea level that will badly affect Asian coastal regions. Fourth, both the quality and quantity of water are at risk due to land-use changes. Finally, deforestation causes stress as forestlands are taken over for settlements, agriculture, and industry.

All these five "Pachuari areas" are directly related to energy consumption. Soil is degraded by energy-based pollution, so is air quality. We all understand the link between fossil fuel and climate change; water is often polluted as a result of energy use, and trees are frequently cropped and burnt for fuel without there being a proper reafforestation programme.

Pachauri argues that poverty is more than a mere lack of income. Poverty, he holds, is people's lack of ability to retain control over their living conditions. Thus, if a community lacks empowerment to live in a way that is sustainable, poverty results. There are of course other factors that affect this but the core of his argument is very compelling as it points out a cycle between environmental degradation and poverty.

It is simplistic to blame markets and private economic activity for environmental problems. They are not the only cause of energy-induced environmental problems. Governments are also to blame and, sometimes just as much to blame as the most evil form of capitalism. There are many areas where governments need to do more, but in many areas it would be better if they did less. Subsidising energy increases environmental pressures. The planned economies of the former Soviet bloc highly subsidised energy and water resources, which ultimately contributed to their very poor environmental records. The industrialised areas of communist Czechoslovakia and East Germany were the worst polluters in Europe and had the worst air quality in Europe. It is not only the planned socialist economies that have caused problems but also nations which have allowed industry to consume energy without any controls. Finally individuals, especially those who live in the high consuming prosperous Western economies, also contribute to the problem.

Against this background it is unsurprising that nations have conflicting interests in environmental energy use. Some need to maintain the standards and quality that they have created; others need to develop. There is inequality between nations and this makes it hard for genuine negotiations to take place because the powerful nations hold all the aces. Institutional structures can make it difficult to find agreement or compromise between international organisations: between the International Monetary Fund and United Nations, for example, or between national sovereignty and the need for an international organisation that has real teeth to enforce environmental change.

In 1993 the World Energy Efficiency Association was founded as a private, non-profit organization composed of developed and developing country institutions and individuals charged with increasing energy efficiency. Its mission is to assist developing countries to access information on energy efficiency, serve as a clearing house for information on energy efficiency programmes, technologies and measures, disseminate this information worldwide, and publicise international cooperation efforts in energy efficiency. The WEEA points out:

"Modern energy can transform peoples' lives for the better. It improves productivity, frees millions of women and children from the daily grind of water and fuelwood collection, and through the provision of artificial lighting can extend the working day, providing also the invaluable ability to invest more time in education, health, and the community. Energy opens a window to the world through radio, television, and the telephone."

It highlights the facts that no country has managed to develop significantly more than a subsistence economy, without ensuring at least minimum access to energy services for most of its people, and that those living in developing countries attach a high priority to energy services. On average, these people spend, it is claimed, nearly 12% of their income on energy.

Providing energy to a population, especially energy created by the combustion of fossil fuels and biomass, will have adverse environmental effects. In rich countries, people are mainly concerned with the global consequences of fuel combustion, because many of its local effects (such as the infamous London "pea-souper" fog) have been controlled at considerable expense by clean air legislation. In developing countries, the local environmental problems associated with energy use remain matters of concern that are at least as pressing as they were in industrialized countries fifty or more years ago. The poor suffer most severely from this type of pollution, because they have no access to better alternatives, and are forced to rely upon the most inefficient and polluting sources of energy, says the WEEA which further argues:

"World population is expected to double by the middle of the 21st century, and economic development needs to continue, particularly in the South. According to the scenarios of this study, this results in a three- to five- fold increase in world economic output by 2050 and a ten- to fifteen-fold increase by 2100. By 2100, per capita income in most of the currently developing countries will have reached and surpassed the levels of today's developed countries. Disparities are likely to persist, and despite rapid economic development, adequate energy services may not be available to everyone, even in 100 years. Nonetheless the distinction between ``developed'' and ``developing'' countries in today's sense will no longer be appropriate. Primary and final energy use will grow much less than the demand for energy services due to improvements in energy intensities. We expect a one and a half- to three-fold increase in primary energy requirements by 2050, and a two- to five-fold increase by 2100."

If the WEEA is right, the consequences for those alive in the next century will be drastic.

The mechanism that the rich countries use to assist the development of poorer countries is loans and finance from the World Bank. This important institution attempts to provide effective development assistance to poorer countries and therefore is likely to have an immense impact upon energy issues in the world.

Founded in 1944, the World Bank provided US$17.3 billion in loans to its "client" countries in 2001. It works with government agencies, nongovernmental organizations, and the private sector to formulate assistance strategies. More than 180 member countries own the World Bank and have the power to control its ultimate decision-making.

Its main focus is on helping the poorest people and the poorest countries.

The World Bank's energy strategy is therefore vitally influential. The World Bank effectively decides which projects to fund and which to abandon. Its role is critical and its energy strategy of fundamental importance to the future.

There are three key parts to its strategy: policy assistance, knowledge management, and support for a variety of specific investments that help environmentally responsible policies, and support environmental best practice. The World Bank declares:

"The specific policy areas in which we will seek to engage clients and stakeholders are:

- *Adopting a broad range of policies that target the principal sources of pollution across sectors, that are aimed at tangible improvements in environmental quality ... and that balance the cost of compliance with environmental benefits. At the energy-environment interface, maximum benefits can only be captured by cross-sectoral policy making. Given the fragmented nature of sectoral decision-making in most of the Bank's client countries, making progress in this area is a considerable challenge.*

- *Accelerating the substitution of traditional fuels by modern energy and promoting new energy technologies, including renewables, by removing barriers to the development of their markets.*

- *Strengthening monitoring and enforcement capabilities for mitigating the environmental impacts of energy production and use across all levels of government, with a focus on local government and an increased role for communities and civil society.*

- *Promoting the restructuring of energy sector institutions and ownership as a focus of the energy-environment policy agenda, in order to capture the important environmental gains that energy sector reform involves. For example, pricing reform can enable proper reflection of the environmental costs of energy use and, along with market liberalisation, can encourage improved energy efficiency.*

The "clients" of the World Bank – the poorer nations that borrow - will inevitably consume more energy as they get wealthier. The World Bank's approach is different from Dr Pauchari's but both approaches agree on at least one thing – the need to promote energy efficiency and renewables is critical. For poorer people to become less poor and for the whole planet not to become impoverished it is of paramount and central importance that we have energy that is sustainable.

Chapter 11

Energy of the future

We have seen that the traditional fossil fuels of oil, coal and gas provide us with major sources of energy. Coal was the first energy source that transformed Europe and North America and laid the foundation of the Industrial Revolution over two hundred years ago. At the beginning of the last century oil became important and the development of the internal combustion engine created greater and greater demands for oil until it became central to our energy requirements.

It is still essential today, and as a result huge power and control is vested in multinational corporations and some relatively small oil-producing states. Gas became important in the United Kingdom when large gas fields were found under the North Sea. Lastly nuclear power became important in the middle and later parts of the last century.

The new century will be the century of renewable energy. We note Professor Stephen Hawking's warnings that unless humankind colonises planets in outer space, it will have no future, due to global warming. The danger of global warming may be that it is simply irreversible, or more likely, that humankind will not heed the warnings and the dangers and will do nothing to reverse the burning of fossil fuels and other malpractices which are leading to a crisis that will affect the whole planet.

We believe that it is undesirable for energy to be controlled by multinational corporations or by sovereign states, whether large or small. Energy is so important, in that it is needed for our health, comfort, employment, and security and well-being, that it should be diversely controlled and capable of being obtained from as many different sources as possible.

Government policy in the United Kingdom has always sought to achieve diversity of supply. With current developments it will, in the near future, be possible for the United Kingdom to be supplied with energy from many diverse sources, none of which could be easily controlled or threatened by monopolies or other sovereign states.

There are nine relatively new, environmentally friendly ways of creating energy, which will over the next few years prove as significant and as important to humanity as the traditional forms of energy production. These are Vacuum Collectors, Solar Panels, Fuel Cells, Photovoltaic Cells, Wind Turbines, Tidal and Wave Power, Ocean Thermal Power, Geothermal Heat Pumps and Biomass.

Aditionally it is possible to combine these individual technologies so that, for example, solar collectors and cells can be used in complementary ways. We shall examine each of these modern methods of producing energy. The important question that we must address with each of these technologies is not what is possible, but what is practical. Does it do what it says on the box?

Chapter 12

Vacuum collectors

Although vacuum collectors are fairly simple, the concept of a vacuum is relatively new, in terms of scientific history. One German scientist played a particularly important part in proving that vacuums exist and in inventing apparatus for creating vacuums. The story begins in 1602, when Otto Guericke was born in Magdeburg, close to Hanover, where his family had lived for three centuries. This was a time of great scientific exploration. Guericke studied law at Leipzig University, which he entered when he was 15 years old, then at Helmstadt, and finally in Leiden in Holland. Like many educated young men of that time he studied mathematics, geometry and mechanics and found that he had an aptitude for what we would now call engineering.

After touring England and France he resettled in Magdeburg and planned the rebuilding of the city using his engineering skills. When he was in his mid-forties he was elected Mayor and then entered the most fruitful phase of his scientific career.

He was a great inventor. He invented an air pump, a water barometer and a manometer. The invention of the air pump, however, was crucial because at that time he was looking for ways to create a vacuum. He managed to create vacuums in glass and metal vessels, provided that the material used to make the vessel was strong enough to stand the outside air pressure. His experiments impressed the Elector Friedrich Wilhelm who asked Guericke to arrange a demonstration of a vacuum.

Guericke built a globe made up of two small hemispheres fitted with leather washers. It was slightly larger than a basketball and could be pulled apart by a small child. He then used his air pump to evacuate the globe (creating a vacuum inside it) and harnessed eight horses to each hemisphere. After a great deal of strain the horses eventually managed to pull the small hemispheres apart. As the globe was pulled apart there was a loud frightening bang.

He also proved that inside a vacuum, candles would not burn, animals could not live and a ringing bell could not be heard. These were unknown qualities of a previously unknown property – the vacuum.

The Emperor ennobled Guericke, and Otto became von Guericke. He died in 1686 at the age of 84. Much later, the University of Magdeburg was named in his honour. Without his work we would not be able to create vacuum tubes today.

Later, an Irishman, Robert Boyle, improved on Guericke's invention, working jointly with Robert Hooke in London. Hooke and Boyle invented an air pump they called the pneumatic engine. Boyle later became famous for his law defining the way in which a given volume of air varies inversely to the pressure on it, but alas, no university has been named in Boyle's honour.

Building on the work of von Guericke and Boyle, the most popular use of evacuated vessels was, for many years, the humble vacuum flask. For a long time the technology was only operated in laboratories for experimentation. Gradually other practical uses were found for it. It was applied to degassing molten metals, electronic beam smelting and welding, vaporising metals so that the vapours could be applied as coatings, freeze drying, pharmaceutical freezing, manufacturing electric light bulbs, electronic valves, gas discharge valves and spectrometers. The technology was also invaluable in Ion source technology, particle accelerators and vacuum spectrographs. Other important applications were in the fields of low temperature physics, plasma, nuclear fusion and space simulators.

At this time the engineering concern of Dornier Systems, which was producing space satellites, was using its thermodynamics department to calculate the heat balance of satellites. This was important work because, during a space mission, satellites are exposed to ultra high vacuums, solar radiation, deep space temperature and self-generated waste heat.

The Dornier team thus knew all about vacuums and solar radiation and the radiation by light on surfaces. The 1974 energy crisis caused by the rocketing price of oil inspired them to use their knowledge to create energy saving applications for use on earth, rather than in space.

At this point, it is helpful to expand on the description of the nature and activity of the sun, which we considered earlier. The sun is the source of all our energy. It is a sphere made up of intensely hot gases, the center is unimaginably hot and has a density about 100 times that of water. The sun's activity is like that of a continuous fusion reactor, constantly emitting energy by radiation. The energy is produced by the fusion (or collision) of matter at its core; the gases of which the sun is composed contain the fusion reaction and are themselves held together by gravity. The energy is pushed to the outer zone of the sun by convection and from there is radiated out into space at various wavelengths. That part of it that reaches our planet is received in two forms. Beam radiation is radiation received from the sun without being scattered by the earth's atmosphere. Other energy is received in a form that is scattered by the atmosphere and is referred to as diffuse radiation. The scattering occurs when the radiation passes through air molecules, water and vapour droplets and dust. The two forms together are known as total solar radiation.

Above the earth's atmosphere insolation is constant and reliable. However, here on the earth's surface the amount of radiated energy received at any given point is determined by the factors we have just mentioned and in addition several others. These are the spherical shape of the planet, the stage of its rotational and seasonal cycles and the latitude of the point in question. Every year comprises about 8760 hours (more in leap years). Half of these hours are spent in nighttime at any particular location and of the remaining time somewhere between 1300 and 2000 hours are spent in sunshine. Clearly then sunshine is not always going to be present as a source of energy, however solar radiation, which must not be confused with sunshine, is present during all daylight hours and in all weather conditions. It is solar radiation which proved to be the crucial potential source of energy.

The Dornier team's first invention was a flat plate solar collector to which a selective coating invented by the team was applied. Trials proved that these collectors were unsuitable for what was then thought to be the main market – deserts and tropical zones. They were badly affected by corrosion and this degraded performance.

When they tested their collectors in North Germany they were disappointed with the results. Performance was just not good enough. There was not enough insolation to power the flat plates, ambient temperatures were low and heat losses by wind and weather were high. It became obvious to the team that only vacuum tubes could produce the right results.

The designers of the final product had to take two problems into account. First of these was to use the properties of insolation. Traditional solar panels did not convert radiated solar energy into heat, but rather used direct heat from the sun. They only worked on sunny days in hot weather. Solar collectors that ignore radiated energy have almost no application in most parts of the world. Solar radiation, on the other hand, is present and measurable on cloudy and cold days and is available in sufficient quantities to be useful at all latitudes and in all climates. The second problem that the engineers needed to address was not how to collect the energy –once they had determined that there is sufficient radiation in daylight hours, even at northern latitudes, for useful applications. It was how to prevent most of the energy radiating straight back out of the panels. The team found that vacuum tubes met each of these requirements.

A key member of the team that developed the vacuum tubes was Peter Schubert, a graduate of Stuttgart University with a doctorate in Nuclear Engineering and Thermodynamics. Between 1973 and 1978 he worked first for Dornier, then DaimlerBenz Aerospace, as an engineer researching and developing solar-powered systems. He led solar projects in many countries and ultimately became Head of the Solar Energy Department for DaimlerBenz Aerospace. He has run solar projects in such places as Mexico, Egypt, and China while becoming convinced of the suitability of solar energy for northern European countries. He retired from DaimlerBenz in 1998 and in 1999 joined Genersys as Engineering Consultant. The present quality and performance of Genersys's vacuum tubes is very much due to the vision and work to which Peter Schubert has devoted his life.

At an early stage Schubert and his team realised that their solar collectors must fulfil two essential requirements in order to succeed in northern Europe. First, the part of the collector that absorbs energy must be selectively coated in order to absorb the light as completely as possible. We have seen that after the surface absorbs light, the light is transferred to heat. A heated absorber surface tends to emit long wave radiation in the infrared range of the spectrum back into the surrounding atmosphere. This causes heat loss. However, if the absorber surface is coated with a selective coating it gains properties of high absorption and low emission of radiation. This is expressed as the ratio of absorption:emission. High grade selective coatings have absorption: emission ratios of between 10 and 15:1; they absorb a lot and emit little. The radiation that has travelled through space to our solar collector is actually absorbed by a black-body or absorber plate. This is a black or navy blue plate inside the vacuum tube or the solar panel. (Although the absorber plate is called a blackbody, it is not black or navy blue, it just appears so to the human eye.) The blackbody collects the radiation and, because of the efficiency of its design, emits as little of it as possible in the form of reflected radiation. But the energy has to go somewhere. The blackbody, besides being a very good absorber of solar radiation, is equally good at converting the solar radiation into heat. If the black-body is insulated from its surroundings it will in time cause any adjacent heat pipe to reach the same temperature. This leads to the second requirement: they needed to design a collector where the radiation of the sun is converted into heat, while long wave radiation back into the surrounding atmosphere is kept as low as possible. (The process by which the light absorbed is converted into heat is referred to as "heat transfer".)

If the heated absorber surface is surrounded by air, heat is also lost through the ordinary processes of conduction and convection. Therefore the collector must be equipped with highly efficient heat insulation to ensure there are no convection and heat conduction losses (that is to say to prevent the heat being dissipated into the atmosphere). Cold weather and cold wind can both prevent solar collectors from working efficiently.

Whilst in highly specified solar panels like the Genersys 1000, the insulation will be in the form of fibreglass filling, in the most efficient systems, a near perfect vacuum (the Genersys 1350 and the 1450Kr) and a perfect vacuum (the Genersys 1650) provide the most effective form of insulation, thus preventing almost all of the heat escaping except through the heat pipe.

The team found that vacuum tubes met each of these requirements almost perfectly. They had, using elementary physics in an imaginative and scientific way, addressed the two key problems in using solar energy.

The collectors comprise a heat pipe fixed onto an absorber inside a vacuum tube. The absorber collects the insolation energy and converts 96% of it into thermal energy, or heat. Heat tubes, or heat pipes are also a development of the satellite aerospace industry. Most of the heat cannot pass out of the vacuum, although a tiny fraction is radiated out despite the low emission values of the selective coating. Most of the heat remains trapped inside the heat tube where it is pumped into a hot water supply, either eliminating the need for a separate energy source for heating water in good daylight conditions, or acting as a booster to an existing system and thereby saving energy.

By making the vacuum tube of such good quality, that is, by applying such a very high vacuum as to make the collector almost unaffected by surrounding temperatures and winds, the team designed a product that efficiently collected the energy of the sun and retained it for use. So the vacuum solar collector was developed. In fact, in its simple earliest form the product involved no special patents – the technology is now mature and is founded upon elementary physics. Having created a workable efficient vacuum collector the Dornier group needed to market the product. They formed a partnership with Prinz, who had also already undertaken some research in this field; the resultant partnership was called Dornier-Prinz.

Subsequently DaimlerBenz Aerospace (as they were called then) acquired Dornier-Prinz and assembled a formidable team of physicists and engineers who, using their expertise in space and vacuum technology, ultimately developed vacuum tubes of high technical standards.

On average in the United Kingdom, it is calculated that insolation is sufficient to provide 100% of hot water requirements in June and July, 95% in May, over 80% in April, August and September, 60% in March and October but less than 40% from November to February. Conditions will vary from place to place, but with a normal collector installation 60% to 80% of the hot water supply should be achieved by purely solar means. Even in the dark cold days of winter the collectors still work, but not as efficiently as in summer. This is because in the United Kingdom there is much less daylight in winter than in summer, as compared with places closer to the equator, and also because the angle of the sun is much lower in the sky in the winter and that makes the light received weaker in intensity. Although the vacuum collectors will not be contributing the massive 4 to 5 kWh per square metre of output that they achieve on a bright 12 hour summer's day, they will nevertheless contribute significant amounts of free hot water.

Although the principles are simple the efficiency and installation of the system is not always straightforward. Factories, offices, hospitals, schools and other institutions can all benefit from solar collectors although those installing the systems require thorough training. Installations in existing domestic housing also need skill and experience in order to ensure the right configuration is used and that the best results are obtained. In the case of property that is in the process of being constructed, the system can be built in at a substantial cost saving, and the more enlightened builders design solar collectors into their buildings at the drawing board stage.

The common flat plate collectors, known as solar panels, which we discuss more fully in the next chapter, have several important disadvantages when compared with vacuum tubes. Certainly vacuum tubes are more efficient in transient seasons and in using winter insolation. Tubes need less light than panels. Being made of glass they do not rust, corrode or degrade. The vacuum prevents any oxygen or humidity coming into contact with the absorber surface. However, the vacuum tubes have many disadvantages; they operate through a manifold, so that only a small part of the heat exchange fluid comes into contact with the blackbody. Further, they do not provide a pleasing apearance.

Today, the most efficient evacuated solar collectors are made with the best quality glass manufactured to very high specifications. Flaws, such as small fractures or bubbles in the glass, cannot be tolerated. The seals that contain the vacuum must be carefully assembled. Genersys's collectors are manufactured to the highest specifications; its collectors should retain optimum efficiency for 35 years or more. Collectors installed twenty years ago (of a less sophisticated design than those being manufactured for Genersys today) are still providing trouble-free use.

Sometimes, as with every manufacturing process, small faults occur and have to be remedied. The modular design of the tubes has made tube replacement or augmentation practical where a tube has become damaged or, exceptionally, lost its vacuum. Each vacuum tube in an installation is an independent unit and accordingly can be exchanged if necessary.

It is expected that within the next few years technicians will be able to re-evacuate any Genersys tube in situ, making the product even more energy-efficient that it is at present, because the high specification glass which forms the structure of the tube should last for hundreds of years without degradation. When it no longer produces free energy the tube can be re-evacuated or recycled.

Chapter 13

Solar panels

At one time the only system of collecting solar energy that was sufficiently developed for domestic purposes was solar panels. Solar panels (or flat plate collectors) are simply flattish high mounted radiators (usually placed on a flat roof) that absorb the heat from sunlight. Inside the panels are copper tubes containing water or anti-freeze that is heated by the sunlight and then drawn down by the household and used for water heating.

Panels are cheap and can be ideal solutions for places that experience a great deal of hot and consistent sunshine – such as the southern Mediterranean area and the northern part of Africa. Some poor quality panels do not work at all when there is no direct sunshine and are fairly inefficient, but they can present a cheap and effective way of heating water. Although the solar panels are efficient at collecting the energy, much heat escapes out of the panel before it can be used.

Solar panel design has improved significantly so that these systems are now suitable for temperate climates such as those of the United Kingdom, Germany, Holland, Belgium and countries sharing similar latitudes. In particular the world-leading panels made in Slovakia by one of Genersys's German partners, ThermoSolar, have advanced features that assist in retaining as much energy as possible.

The inspiration behind these panels is Johann Kollmansberger, an environmental architect, whose design flair and thorough understanding of the market's requirements is shown in the excellent range of Genersys panels.

The principles of radiated light and heat transfer discussed in the previous chapter apply equally to Genersys's solar panels.

The basic collector, the Genersys 1000, is cased in high quality aluminium/ magnesium alloy and contains just under a litre of fluid in its compression-proof copper piping. The internal pipe-work is insulated. The panel has an absorbing surface of 1.75 square meters made up of an aluminium oxide based layer covered with colloidal nickel pigment for high efficiency absorption. The panel is covered in low reflection, highly transparent white glass that has been pre-stressed and tested for hailstone resistance.

Genersys's top of the range solar panel, the Genersys 1450Kr has a similar appearance to the basic panel, although it is slightly larger and has a larger collector area, but internally there is one key difference. The inside of the panel has been evacuated and filled with krypton gas. Krypton is a colourless, odourless gas that is inert to virtually any element known except fluorine. Special patented connections ensure that the panel is never welded, soldered or secured together by pins or other devices. Upgrade and expansion is easy because the panel is designed with this in mind.

The vacuum created inside the Genersys 1450 Kr is not and can never be as perfect as that created in a glass tube. The panel was accordingly designed with an evacuation valve that can be used to test and renew the vacuum as necessary. After installation, the panel's vacuum should last five or six years at least, but Genersys recommend that the integrity of the vacuum is checked annually along with the heating or hot water system connected to it to ensure optimum performance.

Environmentalists will be pleased to learn that all Genersys products are made out of 100% fully recyclable materials.

The reliability of solar panels during their expected lifetime depends on the long-term stability of their components. Many solar panels age and can corrode. They react to atmospheric humidity, temperature and sulphur dioxide. ThermoSolar's panels are manufactured from lightweight, non-corrodible, high quality aluminium alloy. They can withstand the rigours of pollution and are resistant enough also to withstand accidental damage, storms and adverse weather conditions. They are strong enough to be moved (if necessary) even when they have been built into the fabric of the roof. They are robust and well enough made to be used as a roofing material instead of slates and tiles. Their estimated life span is in excess of thirty years.

There are many products being marketed that are not as sophisticated as the Genersys range. These old fashioned and largely non-technological products do have some benefits, but in modern conditions it is not cost effective to instal them and probably, once the materials used and the effect of corrosion are taken into account, they cause more pollution than they save. If any benefit is to be enjoyed in terms of cost savings and reduced carbon dioxide emissions then only the best quality solar panels with a high-quality engineering provenance should be used.

Chapter 14

Fuel cells

Judge Sir William Grove, a Welshman, invented fuels cells in 1839. His prototype fuel cell worked but seemed to have no practical use until the United States Space Program decided that using fuel cells in their spacecraft would be cheaper than solar power and less risky than nuclear power. As a result NASA developed sophisticated fuel cells to furnish power to the Gemini and Apollo craft.

A fuel cell operates like a battery in that it will produce energy in the form of electricity and heat as long as fuel is supplied. Unlike a battery it does not need recharging, nor will it run down.

The chemistry of a fuel cell is based on simple principles. An electrolyte is placed between two electrodes. The electrodes separate the gases from the electrolyte. The processes take place in the electrodes, which consist of sintered metal or carbon powder. They are porous and equipped with semi-permeable membranes. If oxygen (or air) is passed into the cathode end of the fuel cell and hydrogen (the lightest element) is passed into the anode end of the fuel cell, in principle a hydrogen electrode and an oxygen electrode are established. Facilitated by a suitable catalyst the hydrogen is oxidized releasing electrons so that the anode has a surplus of electrons, which causes a negative charge. The oxygen is reduced in the cathode, consuming electrons, which causes a lack of electrons and consequently a positive charge. By connecting the anode and the cathode, electrons are caused to flow from the anode to the cathode, and electric current is created. The electrons create a separate current. Water vapour is produced as a by-product.

Hydrogen is not an energy source, like coal or oil, but a clean energy carrier, like electricity. It can be stored and converted into different forms of energy. It has been used as rocket fuel, in weather balloons and in oil refining. It is one of the simplest fuels available to us.

Hydrogen remains potentially the cleanest source of power, but the difficulties of extracting, storing and transporting it around (we are all aware of what happened to the hydrogen air ship the Hindenberg) have yet to be fully solved.

At one time it was thought that fuel cells would only run on hydrogen but some research projects, particularly at the University of Pennsylvania, have created a cell which uses the hydrogen naturally occurring in hydrocarbons like petrol, diesel or natural gas. The classic fuel cell image – of a car with a huge hydrogen bag on its roof – has become a thing of the past. The fuel cells presently being tested in cars by Mercedes-Benz use methanol.

Fuel cells provide a very clean form of power. Although pure hydrogen delivers no emissions when used in fuel cells, merely water vapour; petrol, methanol and diesel do deliver some emissions; however, these are significantly less in terms of power generated. This is because the process is chemically based, rather than utilising combustion. Waste products are created, but the amount of pollution is less than 10% of that produced by an ordinary vehicle.

We expect that fuel cells will ultimately have their greatest use in powering motorcars. They would appear to be more powerful than their main alternative – battery powered cars, and more energy-efficient, and would allow vehicles to travel further between refuelling. Car manufacturers expect that within the next few years in a car engine using a fuel cell will be in mass production and will cost no more to produce than one delivering the same power by burning petrol. Although fuel cell technology is still immature, when compared with solar collector technology, scientists should be able to overcome all the teething problems, provided that there are incentives for consumers to use fuel-efficient cars and there is investment into research.

At the moment fuel cells are very expensive to produce in relation to the power that they provide. This was also the case with computers until they went into mass production.

One leading car manufacturers, DaimlerChrysler, expect to have an engine in production by 2004. They have developed a concept vehicle based on the Jeep Commander with a hybrid fuel cell system. In this the engine is powered by a fuel cell and battery; the fuel cell runs on petrol. The Mercedes S class model has a fuel cell as a compact auxiliary power unit. Additionally, work is being developed on the NECAR, a fuel cell van. They have produced four generations of the NECAR so far and the fifth generation NECAR is to be unveiled shortly.

General Motors, in the United States, have developed the Precept concept car. Electricity from the fuel cell drives an electric motor on the front axle. The rear axle is separately powered. GM expect that the Precept will achieve the equivalent of over 100 miles per gallon and that they will go into mass production with a fuel cell vehicle during 2004 or 2005.

Ford are also involved in development of fuel cell driven motorcars. Their TH!NK FC5 – a family sized car – is powered by a Ballard fuel cell which uses methanol. The engine is located under the floor, creating a huge amount of passenger and luggage space.

BMW in Europe have a joint venture with DELPHI Automotive Systems the purpose of which is to develop fuel cell vehicles using solid oxide technology. BMW plans to fit hydrogen fuel cells that will power their series 7 electric saloon cars and fork-lift trucks.

Peugeot Citroën, Renault and Volkswagen and Volvo all have advanced fuel cell projects. Toyota and Nissan plan to introduce their own commercial fuel cell vehicles in 2003. Mazda too have produced a fuel cell concept car.

The prospect of all road transport no longer burning petrol or derv or at least burning only 10% of the amount of fuel that they do at present, no longer polluting the air we breathe, and creating as a by-product simple water, is very attractive. There may be other problems created by pumping excessive water vapour into the atmosphere (and after all water vapour is the most pernicious greenhouse gas) but we all instinctively feel that filling the air with water must be safer for us and for our children than the unkind gases that motor vehicles presently deliver.

Chapter 15

Wind turbines

Humankind has always valued the power of the wind. It has transported sailing vessels from the earliest times. The wind was turning mills to grind corn and wheat in China and Persia 2000 years ago, and Holland virtually owes its existence to the windmills that drained its marshes.

In modern times the real drive to use wind power for producing electricity came from Poul la Cour, a Danish meteorologist, inventor, and high school headmaster, who taught natural science in Denmark at the turn of the last century. La Cour transformed windmills to DC electricity generators in the 1900s. He also patented a mechanical device to stabilise the torque of wind turbines. His inventive mind should be credited with the wind turbine technology, upon which much hope depends for the future. La Cour taught wind energy to Danish "wind electricians". He inspired his students to become wind scientists; some of his best students built wind turbines for FL Smidth, a Danish engineering company, during the Second World War.

In the early 1950s Johannes Juul, chief engineer for a Danish power company, took up his old interest in wind energy that he had acquired during one of la Cour's courses in 1903. Juul was about to retire and wanted to have something to keep him occupied. He built some experimental machines and was the first to connect a wind turbine with an (asynchronous) AC generator to the electrical grid. Around 1956 Juul built the *Gedser* wind turbine. This became the basic design for all modern wind turbines and was for many years the largest in the world. The *Gedser* turbine had aerodynamic tip brakes on the rotor blades that were applied automatically by the centrifugal force in case the turbine turned too quickly. The *Gedser* wind turbine itself was built and financed by a power company

The Danish wind turbine industry is now the world's most highly developed and successful. It started from amateurish beginnings in the 1970s when the oil crisis forced people to consider all alternative forms of energy, but eventually developed into a sophisticated and professional business.

Most wind energy projects in the 1970s began as private schemes, largely pioneered by individuals who based their designs on scaled-down versions of the *Gedser* machine. They produced wind turbines generating no more than 10 to 15 kilowatts of output. One of these pioneers, Riisager, built 30 wind turbines in series.

Meanwhile, a number of innovative designs for smaller machines appeared, and politicians began to take an interest in the new developments, partly due to the energy supply crisis and partly in response to popular opposition to nuclear power in Denmark.

The Danish Parliament legislated that wind-generated electricity should be sold at a fixed percentage of the retail price of conventional electricity and provided capital grants for installing wind turbines in the 1970s. Unfortunately, this scheme was finally abolished in 1989.

In order to regulate Denmark's quality and safety of turbines Denmark's Risøø National Laboratory , (originally established for nuclear power research) employs scientists and engineers in aerodynamics, meteorology, structural dynamics and other related research. The important work done there ensures the reliability of modern wind turbines. This is rightly a matter of public concern in Denmark where there is a healthy and vigorous lobby for all "green" issues.

In the early 1980s the Danish power companies built two experimental machines, one *pitch regulated* and one *stall regulated*, of 630 kW each. For their time these machines were very large compared with the conventional 10 to 25 kW commercial designs. Much larger designs were being researched in Sweden, Germany and the United States. In the 1980s, the State of California began a programme of support for wind energy development. Danish manufacturers, being by far the most experienced in this field, became the leading suppliers. The Californian market expanded dramatically, and volume production of wind turbines began.

Wind turbines operate in fluctuating, relatively slowly moving air, using aerofoils to regulate the power output from the rotor blades. They are built in such a way as to reduce noise as much as possible. Modern wind turbines are three-bladed; an electrical motor keeps the rotor position upwind (that is to say on the windy side of the rotor pole).

Wind turbines have grown dramatically in size and performance during the past 15 years. The early machines of 25 kW with a 10.6-metre rotor diameter may still be found in Denmark. Today the most widely sold turbines have a rated power output of 750-1000 kW, and a rotor diameter of 48-54 metres. The largest machines commercially available are 2,000 kW machines with a 72-metre rotor diameter placed on 70-80 metre towers. Each 2,000 kW machine produces more energy than 135 old, 1980 vintage machines. Thus productivity has increased rapidly. Wind energy co-operatives and individual farmers own more than 80% of the 5,700 wind turbines in Denmark. 100,000 Danish families own wind turbines or shares in wind co-operatives.

Today, wind energy can compete with coal and nuclear energy on average kWh costs. The cost of wind electricity depends heavily on the average wind speed at the turbine site, because the energy content of the wind varies with its speed. Wind turbines should last for 20 years and maintenance and running costs are low. Wind energy today provides 12% of Danish electricity consumption. A target of 16% has been set for 2003. In the year 2030 wind generated electricity will, it is hoped, provide 40 to 50% of Denmark's needs.

We cannot help but admire the Danes. They have invented and exploited a carbon dioxide free method of generating electricity. Export of the wind turbines and their technology has provided employment as well as environmental benefits. Although people complain about the sight of huge wind farms, it seems to us that the alternative, large fossil fuel power stations, is less attractive and more damaging.

In the near future wind farms will be located on the sea. Land is expensive to use, especially in northwest Europe and there are significantly higher wind speeds at sea. The wind at sea is often more stable with less turbulence and less wind shear. This makes it possible to use cheaper turbines, which should last longer. It is believed that sea-based wind farms will have no adverse effect on bird or aquatic life.

There is a sad footnote to the story of wind turbines in the United States. At the height of the oil energy crisis in the 1970s many forward looking Americans sought to develop wind power. They acquired the best Danish windmill technology and built wind farms to generate cheap electricity. When the price of oil reached its pinnacle no-one doubted the wisdom of this, but as the price of oil fell, so many acres of wind farms became disused. Oil became so cheap that it was not worth maintaining the windmills. Many of them still stand in the fields of California with their engines seized and rusted, incapable of generating any power while the energy greedy United States, comprising just 4% of the planet's population, produces 25% of its carbon dioxide, as we have seen.

Chapter 16

Tidal and wave sources

Wave power is waterpower created by the wind and the wind is created by the sun. Like most forms of energy on our planet, energy from the sun is converted into wind power and the winds create the waves. The energy in waves is significant and could make an important contribution to the world's energy supply if we could discover an economical way of extracting it. The tides, caused by a mixture of gravity, the pull of the sun and the moon and the Earth's centrifugal force, contain enough energy to produce 400 GW worldwide if we limit our use of the tides to places that have a tidal range of four metres or more. It is a shame, therefore, that wave and tidal power are so hard to extract.

Although work on wave power commenced in Japan in 1945, the real impetus for research, as with most of the other renewable technologies, came with the oil crisis in the 1970s. Work carried out in Norway and in the United Kingdom enabled more and more efficient designs to be conceived. In 1982 the first tentative British designs were produced. These take various forms, but all of them involve water pressure, which is converted in special turbines, into electricity.

So far the technology has produced self-powered buoys for use in navigation and weather monitoring. Power plants that use waves, built in Kaimei, Japan, and near Tsuruoka City, also in Japan, have proved disappointing in that their electrical output has been more expensive to produce, and, when produced, has actually been substantially less, than was originally predicted.

In 1974 Professor Stephen Salter and his colleagues invented the Salter Duck at Edinburgh University, so called because it resembles the head and beak of a duck. The duck is positioned (with others) parallel to incoming waves, so that the beaks face them. The force of the waves causes the ducks to pivot and the pivoting drives a hydraulic pumping system that powers a generator.

In Madras, India, the Indian Institute of Technology has built a wave energy plant that generates 25 kilowatts for the four months when the sea is relatively calm and 75 kilowatts when the sea is rougher. In the monsoon season it can generate as much as 120 kilowatts. The success of this plant has encouraged the local authorities to design others that will be larger.

In 1985 Kvaerner, the Norwegian engineering company, built a wave plant 18 miles north of Bergen, producing up to 500 kilowatts. It performed reliably for three years until severe storms destroyed it in December 1988. A smaller plant is functioning elsewhere in Norway.

The highest concentration of wave power can be found in the areas of the strongest winds, that is to say between latitudes 40 degrees and 60 degrees in both the northern and southern hemispheres, on the eastern sides of the oceans. The United Kingdom is thus one of the best situated places for the extraction of wave power, but even here large-scale projects have been shelved for the foreseeable future as they are thought to be uneconomic.

A 100-kilowatt system has been installed on Islay in the Hebrides and the system has been connected to the National Grid. Researchers at Coventry Polytechnic have designed a clam type of device that they believe can generate up to 2 megawatts.

Tidal energy is easier to convert than wave energy. In the right coastal environments, usually at the entrances to large estuaries, tidal resonance occurs. This produces a far greater than average tidal range. Good examples are at the Bay of Fundy, Canada, (this has a mean tidal range of 10.8 metres, the largest in the world), and in the Severn Estuary (with a mean range of 8.8 metres). Tidal energy technology is largely conventional and has been tried before in other areas on a smaller scale.

The feasibility of extracting power from the tides in the Severn Estuary was explored in the 1970s but shelved as being uneconomical. However, today there are proposals for a tidal power plant, which, if built, could produce an estimated 8,600 megawatts incorporating 216 turbines – this would be roughly 7% of the United Kingdom's total electricity demand.

The only major tidal power stations in operation today are the 240 MW facility in St. Malo, France, finished in 1966 and comprising a large range of experimental facilities, and a 20 MW unit in the Bay of Fundy, Canada, dating from 1984.

Neither wave nor tidal power is cheaper to produce than conventional power sources. Wave and tides cannot produce steady rates of electricity at peak demand times, and the energy cannot be stored conveniently or economically.

The development of wave power is not proceeding as quickly as it should. In Britain, (which should be in theory one of the best countries in the world for exploiting wave and tidal power) a research group was formed during the energy crisis of 1976, but the research was shelved in 1983 when it became apparent that no large-scale plants would be economic in the short term.

While wave energy is used successfully in very small scale applications, such as powering lighthouses or navigation buoys, its short term prospects as a major contributor to large scale energy production seem to be economically almost ruled out.

In conclusion, until we accept that we cannot continue to push carbon dioxide into the atmosphere, and until we are forced to recognise that cost cannot only be measured in monetary terms, the likelihood of tidal or wave power playing any significant role is virtually nil.

Chapter 17

Ocean thermal power

The ocean covers two thirds of the earth's surface. It absorbs huge amounts of energy from the sun every day. It is estimated that the same amount of energy as is contained in the whole of the world's oil reserves, (all one trillion barrels of it), is absorbed by the oceans in the tropical areas every week. If we could harness merely 20% of the power latent in the oceans, it would probably produce enough electricity to power Europe and North America. It comes as no surprise, therefore, that people have tried to use some of this renewable energy.

In 1881 d'Arsonval, the French physicist, proposed that the differences between sea level seawater and deep-sea seawater could be used to generate power. He designed a closed cycle system.

In 1929, a French engineer, George Claude, constructed a machine on the coast of Cuba that took the warm surface water and put it into an evaporator. The pressure was lowered causing the water to vaporise. The vaporised water was forced through a turbine where it produced 22 kilowatts of electricity. Cold water was piped up from lower ocean depths to cool the vaporised water so the cycle could begin again. Although Claude's machine worked, the pipe that collected cold water at lower depths kept breaking during stormy weather.

In effect, ocean thermal energy conversion merely converts solar radiation to electric power. Converters use the ocean's natural thermal differences to produce a power generating cycle. As long as the temperature between the warm surface water and the cold deep water differs by about 20° Celsius, a system can produce a significant amount of power.

Most ocean thermal energy converters are designed to create electricity in warm, tropical waters. Warm water can evaporate liquids that boil at very low temperatures such as ammonia or freon. The steam produced by the evaporation is forced through turbines to create electricity. The ammonia or freon gas is then put in a storage tank into which cold water from the ocean floor has been forced, to turn the gas back into a liquid that in turn evaporates again, and so the cycle continues.

Modern designs for ocean thermal converters are still largely experimental and can only produce modest amounts of power. The largest so far is off Japan: it makes 100 kilowatts of electricity. Another converter off the coast of Hawaii produces 50 kilowatts of electricity.

The places that achieve the best results for ocean thermal installations are those with narrow shelves and very steep offshore slopes. Ideally the ocean floor should be smooth. This enables there to be a short cold water pipe run that is more efficient than long pipe runs. It is also possible to build the power plant inland, well away from the shore. This would provide some protection against storms at sea that can damage apparatus.

The main problem with building power plants on land is wave turbulence in the surf zone by the edge of the sea. Unless the power plant's water supply and discharge pipes are buried in protective trenches, they will be subject to extreme stress during storms and prolonged periods of heavy seas. The inevitable long pipe runs are also a disadvantage in losing energy.

It is theoretically possible to locate plants on oil rig style mountings on part of the continental shelf with a depth of 100 metres. The plant could be built onshore, towed to the site, and fixed to the sea bed. These plants would suffer from the disadvantages of high building and maintenance costs and high costs of getting the power generated on to shore.

Ocean thermal power is very promising as an alternative energy resource for tropical island communities. Places like the Seychelles, Benin, Kenya, Cuba and the Caribbean Islands rely heavily on imported fuel. Ocean thermal plants in these places could provide cheap power, as well as desalinated water and a variety of marine crops. It seems to us, however, that the technology is still very immature and it is hard to see any real progress emerging in this field for decades. The real problem is an engineering one. There are some factors that limit what can be done. There are very low levels of efficiency for thermodynamic reasons, which are expressed in the equation stated by *the Carnot Process*. The reasons relate to the small difference between the surface temperature of the sea and the temperature of the water at the seabed. Temperature differences in a range of less than 20° Celsius require an extremely large heat exchanger. This makes it impossible to gain energy efficiency, in theory, of more than 7%, while in practice, the real efficiency level is much lower.

Chapter 18

Geothermal heat pumps

The Romans used geothermal springs for bathing and cooking. In 1881 the King of Hawaii, David Kalakaua met with the American inventor of the electric light bulb, Thomas Edison. The King wanted to find out if the steam from Hawaii's volcanoes could be used to generate electricity for Honolulu. Nothing happened for 96 years until April 1976 when a turbo generator was installed to tap into steam at a depth of nearly 2000 metres. Eventually, 25 megawatts of generating power was created – the first form of geothermally generated electricity. Iceland has tapped its geothermal springs for over 70 years, using the heat for central heating and to provide hot water, but not for generating electricity.

The real future for geothermal energy, however, lies with heat pumps. These work anywhere in the world and do not depend upon a suitable hot geothermal spring being located nearby.

Geothermal heat pumps constitute, like solar collectors, cost effective and environmentally friendly technology that uses no fuel. They move heat from the earth into a building (to heat the building) or from a building into the earth (to air condition the building). Although some electricity is used to operate the pumps, fans and compressors, the amounts used are not significant compared with the amounts that would be required to heat or air-condition the house by conventional means. A typical electrical heat pump will just need 100 kWh of power to turn 200 kWh of freely available heat from the environment or waste into 300 kWh of useful heat.

The efficiency of heat pumps lies in the fact that they use low temperature heat created from renewable energy sources. Heat pump systems usually produce twice as much heat from the same amount of fossil fuel by using it to enhance the renewable energy of the land or the sun. Because heat pumps consume less energy than conventional heating systems, their use reduces harmful gas emissions, such as carbon dioxide, sulphur dioxide and nitrogen oxides.

How do heat pumps work? Heat is transferred naturally from warmer to colder temperatures. Heat pumps, however, can force the heat flow in the opposite direction, using a relatively small amount of energy, usually in the form of electricity. Heat pumps can transfer heat from natural heat sources in the air, ground or water, or from man-made heat sources such as industrial or domestic waste, to heat a building or an industrial application. Heat pumps can also be used for cooling.

Almost all heat pumps currently in operation are either based on a vapour compression, or on an absorption cycle. The great majority of heat pumps work on the principle of the vapour compression cycle. The main components in such a heat pump system are the compressor, the expansion valve and two heat exchangers referred to as the evaporator and the condenser. The components are connected to form a closed circuit. A volatile liquid, known as the working fluid or refrigerant, circulates through the four components.

In the evaporator the temperature of the liquid working fluid is kept lower than the temperature of the heat source, causing heat to flow from the heat source to the liquid, so that the working fluid evaporates. Vapour from the evaporator is compressed by the compressor to a higher pressure and temperature. The hot compressed vapour then enters the condenser, where it condenses and gives off heat that is then used to heat a hot water system, a central heating system or an industrial application. As the fluid leaves the condenser it is expanded to the evaporator pressure and temperature in the expansion valve. The working fluid is returned to its original state and once again enters the evaporator. The compressor is usually driven by an electric motor but if the compressor is driven by gas or diesel engines, heat from the cooling water and exhaust gases is used in addition to the condenser heat, improving the overall energy efficiency.

Industrial vapour compression heat pumps often use the process fluid itself as working fluid in an open cycle and because of this they are sometimes called vapour recompressor heat pumps.

Absorption heat pumps are powered by heat rather than mechanical energy. Absorption heat pumps for air conditioning are often gas-fired, while industrial installations are usually driven by high-pressure steam or waste heat. Absorption systems utilise the characteristics that some liquids or salts have to absorb the vapour of the working fluid. Commonly water is the working fluid and lithium bromide the absorbant; sometimes ammonia is the working fluid and water the absorbant.

In absorption systems, compression of the working fluid is achieved thermally in a sealed circuit comprising an absorber, a solution pump, a generator and an expansion valve. Low-pressure vapour from the evaporator is assimilated by the absorbant. This process generates heat. The solution is then pumped to a high pressure, which forces it into the generator. There, the working fluid is boiled off with an external heat supply at a high temperature.

The working fluid in the form of vapour is condensed in the condenser while the absorbant is returned to the absorber via the expansion valve. Heat is extracted from the heat source in the evaporator where it heats space or water, or is otherwise usefully employed. A small amount of electricity may be needed to operate the solution pump.

An ideal heat source for heat pumps in buildings will have a high and stable temperature, will be available in abundance and should not be corrosive or polluted. Soil and ground water are highly practical heat sources for small heat pump systems, while seas, lakes rivers, rock and waste water are all suitable for use in large heat pump systems. Air from the surrounding atmosphere, although commonly used, is still a greatly underexploited source. We shall examine all these potential sources in turn.

Air at ambient temperature is free and widely available. Air-source heat pumps, however, achieve on average a 10-30% lower seasonal performance factor than water-source heat pumps. This is mainly due to the rapid fall in capacity and performance with decreasing outdoor temperature, the relatively high temperature difference in the evaporator, and the energy often spent in defrosting the evaporator and operating the fans. In mild and humid climates frost will accumulate on the evaporator surface where the pump is operating in the temperature range 0-6° Celsius, thus reducing both the capacity and performance of the heat pump system. Reversing the heat pump cycle can defrost the coil but this is often done by other, less energy-efficient, means.

Exhaust air is a common heat source for heat pumps in residential and commercial buildings. The heat pump recovers heat from the ventilation air, and provides water and/or space heating. Continuous operation of the ventilation or air-conditioning system is essential. Some heat pumps are also designed to utilise both exhaust air and ambient air. For large buildings exhaust air heat pumps are often used in combination with air-to-air heat recovery units.

Ground water has stable temperatures of between 4° and 10° Celsius in many places. Heat pumps can tap into this heat source. In open systems the ground water is pumped up, cooled and then re-injected into a separate well or returned to surface water. Open systems suffer from freezing, corrosion and fouling and are not, in our opinion, an ideal use of ground water heat. Closed systems can either be direct expansion systems, with the working fluid evaporating in underground heat exchanger pipes, or brine loop systems. Due to the extra internal temperature difference, brine heat pump systems generally have a lower performance, but are easier to maintain. A major disadvantage of ground water heat pumps is the cost of installing the heat source. If this is not properly (and expensively) done they risk contaminating the water supply or affecting the water table.

Ground-source systems are usually used for residential and commercial applications. Heat is extracted from pipes laid horizontally or vertically in the soil. The thermal capacity of the soil varies with the moisture content and the climatic conditions. Soil temperatures fall during cold weather, when central heating is required. In cold regions most of the energy is extracted as latent heat when the soil freezes. However, in summer the sun will raise the ground temperature.

Rock (geothermal heat) can be used in regions with negligible or no ground water, from bore holes between 100 to 200 metres deep. This type of heat pump is always connected to a brine system with welded plastic pipes extracting heat from the rock. Some rock-coupled systems in commercial buildings use the rock for heat and cold storage. Because of the relatively high cost of the drilling operation, rock is seldom economical for domestic use.

River and lake water are very good heat sources. Unfortunately they suffer from the major disadvantage of low temperatures in winter. Great care has to be taken in designing heat pumps using river and lake water, as it is critical to avoid freezing the evaporator.

In addition to heating water and buildings, heat pumps have many other related functions. Many industries need hot or warm water for industrial processes (such as whisky making) or cleansing processes (bottling plants) as well as hot water for washing, sanitation and cleaning purposes.

Heat pumps operating alone or in conjunction with other energy sources can meet these requirements with significantly less environmental damage and, provided that the government has created the right framework with appropriate incentives, good cost savings.

Heat pumps can operate in a variety of ways. They can provide space heating and/or water heating. They can operate as reversible heaters, cooling the air inside buildings. In the United Kingdom, heat pumped solar systems can meet around 30-85% of a household's annual heating demand subject to local conditions. Peak load needs to be catered for by an auxiliary system, often gas or oil but preferably low cost low peak electricity. In larger buildings the heat pump may be additionally fuelled by air expelled from ventilation systems.

In residential applications room heat pumps can be reversible air-to-air heat pumps. The heat pump can also be integrated in a forced-air duct system or a hydronic heat distribution system with floor heating or radiators as part of a central system.

It is thought, however, that the overall cost of the design and installation of heat pumps makes them still fall short of proper cost effectiveness. The hot water required by industry can still be provided far more cheaply using solar collectors.

Chapter 19

Energy from biomass

We have seen that the United Kingdom relies heavily on the fossil fuels, coal, crude oil, and natural gas, as sources of energy. We have also seen that nuclear energy is important. Fossil fuels take millions of years to form. Such reserves are finite and are being depleted every day by an increasingly energy hungry world. Nuclear energy is potentially problematical because, although the method of producing energy from nuclear fuel may be safe, provided all proper controls are taken (and no one can guarantee that these controls will be rigorously followed for thousands of years), the problem of storing nuclear waste by-products has never been satisfactorily resolved.

The only other naturally occurring combustible energy source that has the potential to be a substitute for fossil fuel is biomass. Biomass comprises all non-fossil organic materials that have an intrinsic chemical energy content. It can be considered as fossil fuel's non-fossilised state. It includes all vegetation (both land and aquatic), trees, scrub, and all waste biomass such as the solid waste that the dust carts collect and the effluent or sewage that our houses release as well as animal wastes, forestry and agricultural residues, and certain types of industrial wastes. Biomass is only renewable in the sense that a relatively short period of time is needed to replace what is used as an energy resource. In this sense it is sometimes better classified as a sustainable energy source.

In common with all energy that we use, biomass comes from the sun. Carbon dioxide is chemically converted into biomass, which in turn is used as an energy source. The process of conversion is called photosynthesis. When carbon dioxide and water are processed with light and chlorophyll, carbohydrate (CH_2O), is created and oxygen is released. For each gram molecule of carbon, about 470 kJ (112 kcal of energy) is absorbed. The usual efficiency level at which photosynthesis captures light and converts it into energy is only around 1%, but as the global energy potential of virgin biomass is very large, it is estimated that the world's renewable, above-ground biomass, that could be harvested and used as an energy resource, is much larger than the world's total annual energy consumption.

According to some research, modern biomass now represents only 3% of primary energy consumption in industrialised countries. However, much of the rural population in developing countries, that is, more than half of the world's population, is still reliant on traditional biomass, mainly in the form of wood, for fuel. Traditional biomass constitutes about a third of primary energy consumption in developing countries.

Biomass can be used in various ways and in various forms. Biomass product can be burnt direct, or after it has been compacted into pellets, used as gas, charcoal or ethanol or used in conjunction with a more traditional fossil fuel.

Pelletising involves compacting biomass at high temperatures and under high pressures. Sometimes biomass particles are compressed in a die to produce briquettes or pellets, which have a significantly smaller volume than the original biomass and therefore have a higher volumetric energy density making them a more compact source of energy. Pellets and briquettes are easier to transport and store than natural biomass. They can be used on a large scale as direct combustion feed, or on a smaller scale in domestic stoves or wood heaters. They can also be used in charcoal production.

Simply burning it creates most biomass energy. The energy produced can be used to provide heat and/or steam for cooking, space heating and industrial processes; or for electricity generation. Small-scale applications, such as domestic cooking and space heating, tend to be very inefficient. There are very large heat transfer losses which can be as high as 90%. More efficient stoves can help to reduce the heat transfer inefficiency.

On a larger scale, biomass such as wood, forestry residues and municipal solid waste, can be burnt to produce process heat or steam to feed steam turbine generators. The size of these generators is constrained by the amount of biomass available in their location. Usually this means that an electricity generator powered by biomass will have a generating capacity of less than 25MW. However, by using a biomass fuel that can be specifically grown locally, such as short rotation plantations or herbaceous energy crops, the generator's capacity can be doubled or trebled.

Chicken litter, a mixture of straw, wood chips and poultry droppings, is another source of biomass. The Thetford Power Station in England will soon be the largest biomass power station in Europe: it will be fuelled by chicken litter.

Large biomass power generation systems can have comparable efficiencies to fossil fuel systems, but this comes at a higher cost due to the need for a specially designed burner to handle the higher moisture content of biomass. However, by using the biomass in a combined heat and electricity production system (or cogeneration system), the economics are significantly improved. Cogeneration is viable at present where there is a local demand for heat as well as electricity.

In Armagh in Northern Ireland a wood fuelled Combined Heat and Power Unit has been operating since 1998. It has been burning wood to provide heating for a local museum and clean electricity for around 400 homes. The fuel is sourced from local woodlands and used saw mill chips, but as there is considerable scope for coppicing in Northern Ireland, it is intended to provide farmers with grants to encourage their planting willow and coppicing the trees as a source of fuel. Wood chips are dried using waste heat from the Combined Heat and Power engine cooling system and then fed into a gasifier where they are heated. Heating takes place in a restricted flow of air, and this converts the chips into a combustible gas.

The gas is then cleaned, cooled, mixed with air and fed into the engine. 10% of the engine fuel is diesel supplied for ignition purposes. The internal combustion of the gas rotates the engine shaft, which is connected to a generator, thus producing electricity.

The engine exhausts contain a considerable amount of heat, which is recovered by diverting them through heat exchangers. The hot water is then pumped to the radiators in the museum for space heating.

The wood fuelled plant produces around 400 kW of heat and 200 kW of electricity at 415 volts. This is transformed to 11kV and carried away on the Northern Irish Electricity grid. The plant is capable of 24 hours a day continuous unmanned operation for 6 days after which the residual charcoal is removed and the wood chips replenished.

This project shows that not only can useful energy be provided using biomass in industrialised countries but also there are very beneficial side effects. Local farmers are encouraged to plant trees and are paid for their crop. Coppicing takes place at seasons when local farmers are often short of work so the seasonal cycles of the crop fit in well with other local activities.

The thermochemical process for converting solid biomass into liquid fuel is called pyrolysis. The biomass is heated in an oxygen-free atmosphere, or partially burnt in a low oxygen atmosphere. This produces a hydrocarbon-rich gas mixture, an oily liquid and a carbon-rich solid residue. The solid residue produced is charcoal, which has a higher energy density than its original fuel, and is smokeless. Traditional charcoal kilns are mounds of wood covered with earth. The carbonisation process is very slow and inefficient in these traditional kilns so more sophisticated kilns are replacing the traditional ones. The pyrolitic or bio-oil produced can be easily transported and refined.

Gasification is a form of pyrolysis, carried out with more air, and at high temperatures in order to optimise the gas production. The resulting gas, known as producer gas, is a mixture of carbon monoxide, hydrogen and methane, together with carbon dioxide and nitrogen. The gas is more versatile than the original solid biomass (usually wood or charcoal). It can be burnt to produce heat and steam, or used in internal combustion engines or gas turbines, which generate electricity.

Biomass gasification is the latest generation of the biomass energy conversion processes. Research indicates that biomass gasification plants can be as economical as conventional coal-fired plants but they are dirty; methods have yet to be found to provide cleaner emissions and this remains the major challenge.

Commercial gasifiers are available in a range of size and types, and can be run on a variety of fuels, including wood, charcoal, coconut shells and rice husks. Again, power output is governed by the supply of biomass. The first gasification combined-cycle power plant in the world is a 6MW facility at Varnamo in Sweden, which is fuelled by wood residues.

There is a large alfalfa gasification combined-cycle power plant in Minnesota, which is the first dedicated crop-fuel plant of its size in the world. Farmers grow alfalfa, a perennial crop. The leaves of the alfalfa plant are used for cattle feed. The alfalfa stems are dried to remove excess moisture. They then undergo the gasification process at the power station where, in the gasifier, the alfalfa stems are converted into a biofuel gas by being heated at very high temperatures.

Burning the biofuel gas generates electricity. The heat given off from the burning gases runs both combustion turbines and steam turbine-generators. The power plant produces 75 Megawatts of electricity. State-of-the-art technology keeps air pollution emissions from the burning gas as low as possible.

Charcoal production is, as we have seen, a form of pyrolysis. Modern charcoal retorts (or furnaces) operating at about 600° Celsius can produce somewhere between a quarter and a third of the dry biomass feed as charcoal. The charcoal produced is 75 - 85% carbon and is useful as a compact, controllable fuel. It can be burnt to provide heat on a large and small scale.

Ethanol can be produced from biomass materials that contain sugars, starch or cellulose. The best-known feedstock for ethanol production is sugar cane, but wheat and other cereals, sugar beet, Jerusalem artichoke, and wood can all be used. Starch-based biomass is usually cheaper than sugar-based materials, but requires additional processing. Cellulose materials, such as wood and straw, are generally readily available but are expensive to prepare.

A process known as fermentation produces ethanol. Typically, sugar is extracted from the biomass crop by crushing it, mixing it with water and yeast, and then keeping it warm in large tanks. The yeast breaks down the sugar and converts it to ethanol. A distillation process is required to remove the water and other impurities. The concentrated ethanol is drawn off and condensed. This can be used as a supplement or substitute for petrol. Brazil has a successful, industrial-scale ethanol project, which produces ethanol from sugar cane for blending with petrol. In the USA maize is used for ethanol production and then blended with petrol.

Using biomass in conjunction with traditional fuel, or cofiring, is an established means of energy production. The biomass involved is usually wood chippings, which are added to the coal with wood as 5 to 15% of the mixture, and burnt to produce steam in a coal power station. Cofiring is currently well developed in the United States but the electricity generating companies are studying the effect of the addition of wood to the coal. They need to know how it affects specific power station performance and whether any problems will arise from its use.

Biomass is a useful form of fuel and in some parts of the world the only form available. It is an attractive source of energy because it is sustainable and renewable and has special features. However it is not a satisfactory answer to the problem of creating energy in a pollution free, benign manner. It is essential to consider the complex interrelations between the important factors in the following areas before we urge the increased use of biomass.

Biomass has a relatively low energy density. Transporting it is expensive and consumes energy. This means that for biomass to be efficient the biomass processing and the energy conversion process must take place close to the source of the biomass.

Incomplete combustion of wood produces organic particulates, carbon monoxide and other harmful gases. If high temperature combustion is used, oxides of nitrogen will be produced.

If natural forests are more widely used for biomass energy there will be more deforestation with serious ecological and social ramifications. This is currently happening in Nepal, parts of India, South America and in Sub-Saharan Africa.

There is a potential conflict between using land for biomass energy and using land for food production.

Some biomass applications are still too expensive to use to generate power compared with, for example new, highly efficient natural gas-fired combined-cycle power stations.

The production and processing of biomass can involve significant energy expenditure, such as on fuel for agricultural vehicles and on fertilisers. This can make the energy created less than the overall energy expended in its production.

Having weighed all these features, what do we find? There are several environmental results of producing and consuming biomass energy. First, burning less fossil fuel is environmentally beneficial. Even using fossil fuel and biomass together as a fuel to generate electricity in dual-fuel combustion or cocombustion power stations, results in fewer undesirable emissions.

Secondly turning household rubbish into fuel reduces the environmental problems of landfill sites. Biogas from landfills, and refuse-derived fuel, industrial wastes (such as "black liquor" generated by the paper industry) can all be burnt to produce heat, steam, and electric power. This must be environmentally beneficial as it disposes of waste usefully, as opposed to consigning it to a landfill site.

Whilst some environmental impacts may be beneficial, this is not always the case. If so called "virgin" biomass is grown specifically for harvesting as a dedicated energy resource, we destroy the biomass in creating energy but grow new biomass to replace it. If more biomass is harvested than is grown, a biomass system is not capable of continued operation as an energy plantation. Furthermore, the environmental impact of burning biomass to generate power is often deleterious because the amount of CO_2 removed from the atmosphere by photosynthesis of the biomass is then less than that needed to balance the amount of biomass carbon emitted from the cropped vegetation. In these cases virgin biomass is not renewable; its use as a fuel results in a net gain in atmospheric CO_2.

Finally, there is a real problem with biomass. Some scientists now consider that biomass burning contributes even more to global warming than fossil fuel consumption. The reasoning is this: because terrestrial biomass is the largest known method of removing atmospheric carbon dioxide, by photosynthesis, overall loss of biomass has a profound effect on atmospheric CO2 build up. Population growth and increased land use due to urbanisation, converting forest to agricultural and pasture land, road building, destroying rainforests and large-scale biomass burning all contribute to the build up of atmospheric CO2 at a rate that is much larger than fossil fuel consumption. Carbon dioxide is certainly the largest single factor responsible for global warming.

How, then, can large-scale biomass energy use be justified? Of course it cannot be justified unless we replant much more than we consume. Every crop must be replaced. We must probably go further than this and create new biomass growth areas. The forests are the largest, long-lived, global reserve of standing biomass carbon and replacing what has been denuded in South American and Africa would go a long way to help restore the ecological carbon balance, and to prevent or reduce atmospheric carbon dioxide build-up. Having replanted the rain forests it would, we believe, be foolish to cut them down again.

Biogas should be distinguished from the rest of biomass energy sources because using biogas does reduce one of the most pernicious greenhouse gases – methane. Most landfills and farms produce methane as an unwanted product. It is 20 times more potent than carbon dioxide as a greenhouse gas. Methane fuelled power stations, such as Holsworthy, Devon, collect slurry from nearby farms and burn the methane gas released to generate electricity. Plants like Holsworthy have an important role to play in alleviating the effect of methane from human activity on global warming.

Chapter 20

Photovoltaic cells

The French physicist, Edmund Becquerel was literally the great grandfather of electrochemistry, in that he was the first of four generations of French scientists who each made significant contributions spanning two centuries. He discovered the photovoltaic effect in 1839. Becquerel observed, while experimenting with an electrolytic cell made up of two platinum electrodes placed in an electricity-conducting solution, that electric current generation increased when exposed to light. He could not explain why.

In 1873, Willoughby Smith discovered the photoconductivity of selenium (an element derived from copper) and, four years later, the photovoltaic effect in solid selenium was noted by Charles Fritts, an American inventor.

Fritts created selenium squares, which he attached to a brass plate. He covered the squares with a transparent gold film and noted that small electrical currents were produced. However, less than one tenth of 1% of the light was converted into electricity, so there was no apparent benefit in the discovery.

It seemed at the time that these eminent scientists were observing and experimenting with no obvious practical end. But often the trial and error of apparently meaningless experimentation and observation leads to discoveries that enhance the quality of life and benefit mankind.

In the 1870s another team of scientists, led by Heinrich Hertz, developed photovoltaic cells made from solid selenium. These could convert light into electricity at an efficiency rate of nearly 2%. In 1905, Albert Einstein published his paper explaining the photoelectric effect. This was based on work by Max Planck, a fellow physicist. His theory was that energy could only be released or absorbed by atoms as atomic radiation in packets called quanta. Einstein used this idea to show why light above certain frequencies shining on a metal caused it to emit electrons. The light shining on a metal behaves as a stream of energy packets called photons, whose energy is proportional to the frequency of the light. (Planck had defined the formula for calculating this.) When the light strikes it, the energy from the photons is transferred to electrons in the metal. If that energy is greater than what is required to overcome the forces which keep the electron in the metal, it will be released. The result is that light with a high enough frequency can knock electrons out of a metal surface.

The displaced electrons are freed to move about, forming a "conduction band," and a hole is left. behind where the freed electrons used to be. They are "harnessed" by the use of semiconductors with different electrical characteristics so that an electric field is generated. This field causes positive and negative charges to move in opposite directions, thus creating electric current.

The only practical use for the technology was for light meters, or so it was thought, and these became commonly employed by photographers from the 1930s. By 1954 scientists working at Bell Laboratories had developed a crystalline silicon cell that performed with an efficiency of 4%. Within six years the conversion efficiency had increased to 14%. The space race gave a further impetus to research; the first US spacecraft used small photovoltaic cells to power radios.

Now, the best cells operate at 21% efficiency, cells of this quality having only very recently been developed, although Boeing have managed to get a 32% rating from one of their experimental cells. This was managed with multijunction cells that sandwich different types of material to maximise the solar energy that can be absorbed. The cells also had anti-reflection coatings to minimise the amount of light bounced off them. They also used light concentrated by a factor of 100. Concentrators are unable to use diffuse sunlight and therefore are only properly effective in dry hot areas, like deserts.

Over half the photovoltaic cells in use today work best in small products where there are low power requirements. The humble solar powered calculator uses a photovoltaic cell, as do watches, small battery chargers and Japanese soft drink vending machines. In rural areas of Europe, photovoltaic cell-powered pumps and drinking troughs are widely usede. In Japan PV-powered insect killers are used instead of insecticides on many farms.

Eventually photovoltaic energy will become more and more important. There are plans in the United States to build a PV generating plant producing enough electricity for a city of 100,000 inhabitants. The plant, naturally enough, will be located in Nevada where it is expected to generate electricity at a cost comparable to oil produced power. The economics of the PV cell do not yet make it feasible to build the same plant in, say, Scotland.

Photovoltaic cell technology is still immature for large-scale use. Its existing uses do save on some pollution by, for example, eliminating the need for batteries in many calculators. Large-scale use is still, however, some way off on the horizon.

Chapter 21

Storing energy

We tend to consume energy as it is created. When humankind discovered fire, the heat was created when it was required. There was inevitably a large amount of wasted fuel. Today there is still too much waste. We burn gas and oil to create energy when we need it but generally burn it inefficiently and wastefully.

The oldest form of energy storage involved harvesting ice from lakes and rivers, which was stored in well-insulated icehouses. Many stately homes in England still have an icehouse in their gardens, built deep underground, in which ice was stored. Indeed, the Hungarian Parliament Building in Budapest is still air conditioned with ice that is brought from Lake Balaton in the winter.

Although, as we have seen, there are many sophisticated forms of energy available to use, there are relatively few methods of storing energy and even fewer ways of storing energy that we have produced.

One of the most efficient energy storage systems, is, of course, fossil fuel. Coal, oil and natural gas in their unused states hold huge amounts of energy that we can release by combustion. We have seen the disadvantages that combusting fossil fuel brings – especially in creating pollution and global warming.

If we use light to create energy then storing that energy becomes relatively inefficient. The most efficient and cost effective form of solar energy is thermal solar, where light is used to heat a medium, usually a water based medium, and then the heat is delivered in the form of hot water or space heating. If we consider solar radiation it is, by its very nature, only available at certain times and, by its very nature, is, in the United Kingdom (as well as most other countries in the World) intermittent. There is substantially less light available when it is snowing or raining heavily. The angle at which the sun's rays strike the United Kingdom in winter provides a significantly lower concentration of solar radiation than is achieved in summer.

Unfortunately, light is generally available when heat is needed less – there is a natural mismatch between consumption of energy in the home and the availability of energy by solar radiation. The peak of solar radiation occurs around noon but the peak in demand for home heating is in the late evening. Most people use hot water at the beginning of the day and at the end of the day, when solar radiation levels are either low or non-existent.

If we can store the energy that we have been able to create from light, we can adjust the mismatch between availability and use to some extent. The traditional way of storing the energy is by storing it as hot water. Modern hot water cylinders are manufactured to very high specifications. Only thirty years ago they were sold without any form of insulation at all, but gradually jacket type insulations were introduced and fitted. Today various forms of materials can be adhered to the copper or stainless steel cylinder, that will hold the heat for long periods. Rather like insulating a loft, installing a high quality hot water cylinder is one of the most cost effective energy saving devices that a householder can use.

Water as a heat storage medium has some excellent characteristics; it is cheap and can transfer heat well. However, it has low energy storage capacity and as a result you need a large volume of water to store a significant amount of energy. Another problem of using water, as a storage medium is that water stores heat over a large temperature range.

Scientists are developing more efficient ways of storing solar created heat. They have found that *phase change materials* such as Glauber Salt and paraffin waxes provide a much higher energy storage capacity than water. These phase change materials deliver energy over a very narrow temperature range and this enables such devices as heat pumps to work more efficiently.

Turkish scientists have been experimenting with stearic acid as a heat transfer and storage medium with highly encouraging results. They have concluded that stearic acid is an excellent heat transfer medium and a very good way of storing energy in domestic solar water heating systems. It has a suitable melting point and a high latent heat level. It melts and solidifies during a heat transfer and storage process and while the heat transfer characteristics are better than the heat storage properties, it does indicate that scientists will probably evolve more efficient ways of storing solar heat than those available to us at present.

Thermal energy storage for space cooling (also known by a variety of names including cool storage, chill storage, or cool thermal storage) can reduce energy costs by allowing energy intensive, electrically driven air conditioning to be operated from current stored during off-peak hours when electricity is cheaper. The storage medium most commonly used is water (stored in the form of ice, chilled water, or an ice slurry), but eutectic salts can also be used. An evaporating refrigerant or a secondary coolant, which is usually a mixture of water and glycol, is used to cool the storage medium.

Originally, cool storage technology was developed for integration with the chilled water-cooling systems that air condition large buildings. More recent cool storage developments have included technologies designed for integration with roof-mounted, direct-expansion cooling systems. Residential-sized cool storage technologies, including smaller versions of the equipment designed for roof mounting, have also been developed, but have proved too expensive for the residential market.

Although originally developed to shift electrical demand to off-peak periods and to take advantage of low-cost off-peak electric rates, many applications can also result in lower first costs and higher system efficiency compared with non-storage systems.

Cool storage systems have not commonly been thought of as energy-saving technologies. No matter how well insulated, thermal storage systems inevitably suffer some energy losses, as energy flows from warmer bodies to cooler bodies. In addition, both cool and warm water is commonly stored in the same tanks – it is cheaper to do this than to install more tanks. Injecting and removing water from different halves of the tank via specially designed piping, to take advantage of natural differences in water density and buoyancy at different temperatures, minimize mixing. Despite this, some mixing and loss of cooling capability takes place.

Chillers in cool storage systems operate at lower evaporator temperatures, which increases energy consumption if other conditions remain the same. This is particularly true for ice storage systems, which require the lowest evaporator temperatures. Energy saving in these systems takes place because the impact of lower evaporator temperatures is partially or totally offset, by the lower condensing temperatures generally experienced when operating chillers at night rather than during the day. Temperatures are around 10° Celsius lower at night than during the day. If the equipment is operated at night, the efficiency of all chillers improves, particularly that of air-cooled chillers, where the condensing temperature is controlled by ambient temperature.

The storage efficiency of chillers is improved by maximising continuous operation at outputs close to full capacity and thus minimizing part-load losses. In retrofit situations, adding storage to meet peak cooling demands allows the least efficient chillers to be turned off or run much less at other times, further increasing savings.

Ice storage systems also present an opportunity for energy savings through cold air distribution. The supply of near-freezing water to air-handling units allows return air to be cooled to a lower temperature. Primary air is distributed at significantly lower temperatures in a cold air system compared with a conventional system. This allows airflow to be reduced by about 40% the colder primary air is fully mixed with some of the return air to achieve the desired room temperature. This allows the use of smaller and cheaper air pumps and ducting, together with lower power consumption by the fans.

In addition to reducing the average cost of electricity consumed, and potentially reducing energy consumption, cool storage can reduce overall cooling system capital and maintenance costs.

Chilled water storage systems rely solely on the sensible heat capacity of water and the temperature difference between supply and return water streams going to and from the cooling load. As a result, the storage volume required is greater than for any of the ice or eutectic salt options. However, using water eliminates the need for secondary coolants and heat exchangers, and standard water chillers can be used without significantly degraded performance or capacity. Water is typically cooled to temperatures that are slightly lower than for a standard chilled water system without storage. The return water temperature may be increased slightly as well, but must remain low enough to ensure adequate indoor humidity control. Maximizing the difference between the temperatures of the cooling water supply and return water maximizes the sensible energy storage capacity per unit of water and minimizes the size of the storage tank necessary. A single tank is usually used to store both the chilled water and the warm water returning from the cooling load. Placing the cooler, denser water at the bottom of the tank, and the warmer water at the top of the tank helps the separation of the two water bodies. Specially designed pipe networks called diffusers allow water to enter and leave the tank without causing significant mixing. The result is a layer of cold water separated from a layer of warm water by a *thermocline*. Chilled water systems tend to work best in retrofit situations, because it is not necessary to modify the chillers, and in very large systems where economies-of-scale lower the cost of the tank. Chilled water storage tanks may also be used as a reservoir for fire-protection water.

A building that the US Department of Energy claims to be the most energy efficient building in the United States, the Centex Building at the International Center in Dallas, relies heavily for its reputation on efficient energy storage. The Centex Building was designed as the corporate headquarters of Centex, one of America's biggest house builders. The building consists of 176,384 square feet of offices and a similar amount of parking space. A key factor in the building's efficiency is its cooling system. The designers have combined large thermal energy storage (they use fourteen Calmac Ice Banks tanks) with a screw-type water-cooled chiller, so that the building's peak electrical load is significantly reduced thus enabling the building to draw power at inexpensive off-peak hours,

Photovoltaic technology, which creates electrical current from light, suffers from greater energy storage problems. Again, the delivery of radiation is usually out of synchronisation with the consumption of electricity, so apart from feeding the current into a grid network, (which provides current when it is not really wanted) the electricity has to be stored.

The traditional energy storage device is a battery. In 1800 an Italian, Count Alessandro Volta, invented a battery by stacking alternate layers of zinc, blotting paper soaked in salt water and silver. He called this a voltaic pile. He attached a wire to the top and bottom of the pile and found that electric current flowed through it. The higher the voltaic pile the greater the voltage.

The process that Volta (gave his name to voltage) discovered turned out to be as follows. Electrons collect on the negative side (or terminal) of the battery. If an electricity conducting substance (like a copper wire) is connected between the negative and positive terminals, the electrons will flow from the negative to the positive terminal very quickly.

Inside the battery, a chemical reaction produces the electrons. The speed of electron production by this chemical reaction (the battery's internal resistance) controls how many electrons can flow between the terminals. Electrons must travel from the negative to the positive terminal for the chemical reaction to take place. Once you connect the battery up, the chemical reaction begins and the energy stored in the battery gradually drains.

It often happens that the person who invents or discovers a process is not the person who exploits it or develops it for commercial use. In the United States in1888 W.W. Gibbs believed that electricity had incredible potential if it were used for lighting, replacing gas. He had previously been heavily involved in the gas lighting business and foresaw that a dependable mechanism for storing power would enable electric lighting companies to provide light when it was needed.

Gibbs formed the Electric Storage Battery Company and bought patents from the French inventor, Clement Payen. His company manufactured one of the first storage batteries, which they called the Chloride Accumulator. Their products provided electric light to Philadelphia as well as powering six new electric streetcars, also in Philadelphia. Their batteries stored the current from dynamos to light Pullman trains; their current drove fans and sewing machines. By 1898, they powered American submarines.

Of course, batteries are a familiar part of every day life. They power all kinds of small consumer goods, from radios to computers, and are used to create the current needed to start car and boat engines. However, they hold relatively small amounts of energy, wear out quickly and they are often made of substances that need to be carefully and expensively disposed of if no collateral environmental damage is to be caused. We therefore need to consider the technological improvements that will enable electrical energy to be stored more efficiently in the near future.

Notwithstanding the losses in transmission of electricity, electric cars would be a great advantage in terms of noise pollution and because such pollution as is created can be more easily disposed of where the energy is generated, rather than where it is used.

Lithium ion batteries are probably the most likely form of new generation battery technology. They will be widely used in larger electric power operations, such as in cars. The batteries have a very high specific energy and a very long life cycle. These batteries will allow a vehicle to travel distances and accelerate at a rate comparable with those of conventional petrol powered vehicles. They are thin and flexible, free from liquid and can be moulded into a variety of shapes.

Aluminium or zinc sacrificial anode batteries may also prove to be great energy storage systems. As these batteries produce electricity, the anode dissolves into the electrolyte. When the anode is completely dissolved, a new anode is placed in the vehicle. The aluminium (or zinc) and the electrolyte are removed and replaced. The used materials are recycled. These batteries are being tested in German postal vans. The batteries carry 80 kilowatt-hours of energy, giving them about the same range as 12 gallons or 50 litres of petrol. In their tests, the German Postal vans have achieved 615 miles at 25 miles per hour.

An aluminium sulphur battery is also being developed and diamond thin films are being studied.

In Sweden, the environmental impact of both the vanadium battery and the lead-acid battery have been carefully studied from the point of view of an average life cycle of these products. The Swedes found that the vanadium battery had a less adverse environmental impact than a lead-acid battery, although the lead acid battery does have many benefits. The net energy storage efficiency of the vanadium battery was greater due to lower primary energy losses during the life cycle. Favourable characteristics such as long cycle-life, good availability of resources and recycling ability, suggest that the vanadium battery could be mass-produced for use in solar photovoltaic storage situations.

By whatever means, improved battery technology would have tremendous environmental benefits. It would make photovoltaic technology more economically viable and would help overcome the problem of delivering energy when it is needed, rather than when it is produced.

Finally we should mention flywheels. Flywheels are different from any other battery technology. They do not store their energy in chemicals, but in their rotating mass. Flywheels are usually made of a composite material and spin at ultra high speeds. Speeds of 65,000 revolutions per minute have been achieved.

Flywheels use a composite instead of steel because of its ability to withstand the rotating forces exerted on the flywheel. To store energy, a flywheel is placed in a sealed container, which is evacuated to reduce air resistance. Because the moving parts are spinning in a vacuum, there is also no mechanical contact with the stationary components of the device. Magnets which are embedded in the flywheel, pass near pickup coils. The magnets induce a current in the coils changing the rotational energy into electrical energy. Flywheels are still at the research and development stage but the results of tests are very encouraging.

Some flywheel power storage systems can provide underground flywheel electricity that will give days of uninterrupted power. They can store energy for years, without any significant loss and are claimed to provide an uninterrupted power supply that is affordable, safe, clean, quiet, needs no maintenance and is environmentally friendly. This seems to make them suitable for short-term emergency power packs, in offices or hospitals, rather than for long term use, but the manufacturers also claim a long life cycle for them, which has a very useful relationship with photovoltaic technology.

Flywheels have tremendous scope for development and when their technology is fully mature they might well be in common use storing the current that daylight creates.

Chapter 22

The Genersys solution

Trying to find an entirely pollution-free source of energy is exactly the same as trying to find a source of perpetual motion. It cannot be done. Every source of energy will have some environmental effect, just as every human on the face of the earth affects the planet in some way. As people trying to solve a problem that people have created, we are not practising alchemy however but seeking proper and sensible solutions. These will not eventually come from any single technology but from a combination of all relevant technologies. There is no point in waiting for a new discovery or an improved version of what exists. It may never happen.

We can examine the case study of how one company, Genersys, has used the principle of adapting existing mature technologies in order to find a solution to the problem of reducing fossil fuel use in the home without compromising the quality of life of the home occupants.

This principle is just as important for the high polluting occupiers of a large, luxurious household as it is for the poor household whose members do not pollute simply because they cannot afford the cost of fuel.

Genersys approached the problem by combining robust existing technologies into a home energy system, which produces energy at about one third of the cost of traditional means and less than one fifth of the emissions of traditional systems.

There are three major components of its home energy system – the Genersys condensing boiler, Genersys solar collectors and the Genersys water store. They are synchronised together for optimum money saving efficiency, building upon the best that the world has to offer. The condensing boiler is assembled in Holland using the best quality stainless steel heat exchangers made in France, the best combustion system, which is made to the highest specification in Italy and the most robust housing and controls, which are made in Germany. The collectors are manufactured in Southern Germany and Slovakia, building on the best aerospace technology, and the water storage system is engineered in Yorkshire and Germany.

By rigorously commissioning the best products from partners who specialise in their manufacture, and by blending them with the most sophisticated electronics, their aim is to create the most efficient and most environmentally friendly home energy system available for the mass market. It will save money and the environment for many years to come by using tried and tested existing technology. The aim is not to create an energy system that is entirely dependent on renewables; that can be done, but at costs that are simply not feasible. The target was to create a mainly fossil fuel free home energy system that can be installed at sensible prices.

For a household paying around £1000 per annum for gas the Genersys Home Energy System might save about £700 each year. The system is modular and can be added to, augmented and serviced at reasonable cost with the minimum of inconvenience.

Let us look at the boiler. Traditional, non-condensing boilers are always very wasteful of energy because they have no efficient way of pumping all the heat they produce into the home. They use a tremendous amount of energy producing latent heat, most of which is discharged into the atmosphere by a flu together with the noxious by-products of combustion. Traditional boilers were designed when fossil fuel was cheap and when no one had made the connection between dirty air and poor health or the connection between heavy fossil fuel use and global warming. They have not changed much in design in the past fifty years.

The Genersys system is different. It has at its heart a condensing boiler – not just any condensing boiler but the best and most efficient available for domestic use in the world. Their condensing boiler discharges hardly any latent heat into the air. Instead, the latent heat that a traditional boiler would discharge into the air is condensed, using superheated steam, and recovered for use as energy to heat the home. The Genersys condensing boiler is so efficient at doing this that it does not need a heavy metal flue but a light stainless steel and PPS plastic one. As a result this system does not waste expensive gas in order to maintain high heat in the home.

However, their condensing boiler does more than this, in fact, much more, when compared with any other condenser. Most of the very best quality range of condensing boilers operate at a typical efficiency of 86% but by using a special and exclusive variable controlled output system, Genersys boilers achieve up to an amazing 98% efficiency rating, the highest available in any product.

In order to achieve optimum efficiency from a condensing boiler we need to be able to control the temperature of the water returning to the boiler. Genersys has achieved this by adjusting the boiler output or the pump speed, or by a combination of both.

When you use gas or electric fires to heat a building, as the outside temperature gets warmer you turn the fire down. This not only allows the room to maintain the right temperature but also reduces energy costs. If you were using gas central heating you would obviously not turn the boiler output down by adjusting the gas valve; because most boilers are not made in a way that the valve can be adjusted by anyone except a qualified engineer.

However, the Genersys system incorporates an integral compensating and modulating digital controller that automatically adjusts the output of the boiler according to the outside temperature and the boiler load requirements. This integrates with a modulating variable speed air pump so that the right amount of air is mixed with the gas for optimum burning efficiency, according to load requirements.

The boiler has a unique combustion chamber where the air and gas mixture is burnt almost without visible flame and with the lowest level of pollution possible. There is no need for a wasteful pilot light.

The final component of this technology is a variable speed water pump, that circulates water through the radiators. A critical factor in any heat exchange operation, like heating a home, is the speed at which the water is pumped.

If the heat exchange medium passes through the system too quickly not enough heat is being pushed into the place where it is needed. If it passes too slowly then the place requiring heat gets too hot, then the system becomes inefficient and, instead barely warm. In engineering terms heating a home is merely a heat exchange operation and the ability to exchange heat through a radiator depends not only on the size of the radiator and the temperature differentials, but also on the speed at which the heat exchange medium is being pumped around the radiator system.

It follows then that if we pump hot water through the radiators too quickly or too slowly there will be an inefficient exchange of energy which is wasteful of fuel; yet that is exactly what happens in almost all home-heating systems. The integrated pump on the Genersys condenser has a variable speed. Not only does this save electricity but it also ensures the system differentials are maintained at the right values for optimum fuel efficiency. This makes a real difference to how much fuel you use.

There is built in frost protection, even if the heating is not turned on, which kicks in at 8° Celsius, as well as an automatic ignition at 5°. When the system returns to 10° the system switches back to idle mode. Many water pumps seize up after a long summer of inactivity. The Genersys system will not because it is programmed to run itself discretely from time to time. So are the fitted mixer valves. These important details have energy efficiency consequences. Components last longer and there are fewer service calls.

The system's combustion can be controlled and monitored using its built in fault diagnosis facility. Engineers can download this onto their laptops and use computerised analysis to achieve optimum energy saving.

This boiler has won numerous awards around the world, including the prestigious German Blue Angel environmental award. It does what every other boiler does, but using a fraction of the fossil fuel that other boilers use, when combined as it is with solar collectors and an efficient water storage mechanism. This replaces the traditional immersion heater. It is larger than the traditional system in order to take advantage of the availability of solar energy. It can be fitted into the loft space, liberating some space in an airing cupboard. It keeps water hotter for longer.

The overall effect of this is not to create an energy system that operates 100% fossil fuel free but is 70% fossil fuel free. That is a massive improvement on a system that is 100% fossil fuel dependent.

People can become rather over-concerned about payback. The concept of payback is not strictly speaking applicable to these solar technologies because payback, by its very nature, depends upon there being a time when the capital asset that is purchased has earned its keep. Homes that are powered by fossil fuel have no possibility of earning a payback. The fuel system exists to provide energy, not to create a cost centre. The gas and electricity company will not in the future agree to provide you with free energy because you have purchased their fossil fuel.

Yet payback appears to be an obsession with many people who consider purchasing solar technology. Consider the example of a renewable technology that saves energy costs over a ten-year period sufficient to pay for itself. The equipment, if made properly, will be long lasting, say, at least thirty years. Some people will say that a payback of ten years is uneconomical. One famous consumer organisation has an oversimplistic attitude to this payback issue. This is flawed thinking. If you want to compare the financial consequences of being either with or without any renewable technology then you must consider the "future free pay" that some renewables can provide. In the example that we have given, the logical way to view the case is that the savings of the renewable technology over ten years pay for the capital cost of the technology; for the next twenty years or more the equipment provides free energy.

When considering these issues do not, as the famous consumer group recommends, simply divide the annual saving into the capital cost. It will give a false picture. Consider also the fact that energy costs are not stable – are they likely to rise or fall in future? If so, by how much? Factor in a servicing saving. If you have installed a good solar water heating system your boiler will not need to work so hard in future. It should need less servicing and last longer. Include these two items in your calculations. Finally, consider the impact of future taxation charges. Is energy created by fossil fuel likely to be taxed more in future or less? Is energy itself likely to cost more or less in the future?

After you have considered all these factors you will be able to find the time after which your energy will be free – your "pay after" time. However, during the whole lifetime of the equipment you will be making a positive environmental contribution, the rewards of which are not costed in mere money.

Chapter 23

Conclusion

We have seen how much energy we need. Energy is a good thing and improves the quality of our lives, but its use at present involves pollution and global warming. These are processes that we cannot fully understand but it is clear that they are harmful and could end life on our planet.

Every source of energy we use, except free energy from the sun or the wind or the ground, involves pollution and emissions. If we choose gas instead of coal we are merely choosing the lesser of two evils.

At one time the prospect of the destruction of the planet by global warming was too far away to cause concern. Now it seems frighteningly close. Each year the calculations by leading scientists of the rate of temperature increase show higher and higher figures. Is it one degree a decade or four degrees? Will the calculations next year prove the figure to be five or six degrees? The chickens are coming home to roost with every flood, heat wave, hurricane and tornado in temperate zones, and in the way that deserts are slowly being created where there was once fertility.

We are an adaptable, inventive species, who have made great progress during our time on this planet. If our time here is to continue then we must divert our efforts into creating energy from the non-polluting sun and not from fossil fuels. We are clever enough to do it.

There are many issues encompassed under the broad heading of energy. There is the need to produce plenty of energy for the sake of our health and comfort. There are the cost issues. There are pollution issues and most important of all there is the issue of global warming.

What should be done? There may be no complete solution to these problems for centuries. We should not wait for one. It may never come. Instead, we must do what we can now.

If you are suffering from an ache that can only be partially relieved, you do not continue to suffer by waiting until you can get 100% relief. You take what relief you can immediately. The fact that one form of energy cannot provide 100% of our energy needs does not require us to reject it. Even if it does no more than provide 30% of our needs from a benign source, solar power helps us solve the problems.

We now know that traditionally generated energy is malignant energy. It creates cancers that are slowly choking life out of our planet.

We must be aware that there is no universal panacea for what ails the planet. Whatever we can do to prevent the burning of fossil fuels will help and if we can reduce our carbon dioxide output by half or two thirds it may be enough to save us.

We cannot hide the fact that cost is a critical issue. Governments do not want to be unpopular. They want to be re-elected. They will not easily adopt the right policies until they are sure public opinion is behind them. In November 2000 senior Government Ministers and senior Opposition figures expressed the view that they were not sure that global warming was, in fact, taking place. By March 2001 the line had changed slightly. The Prime Minister in only his second speech about the environment in four years acknowledged that global warming is happening. The official line had moved to acceptance of the near certainty that global warming was a real problem.

Chapter 24

What happens next

In 1924 Bertrand Russell published a treatise called "Icarus, or the Future of Science". Russell's title sets the scene. If we, like Icarus, fly too close to the sun, we perish. *"Science"*, Russell said, *"without altering men's passions or their general outlook, may increase their power of gratifying their desires"*. Russell was unsure whether, in the end, science will prove to have been a blessing or a curse to humankind.

In Russell's thinking science determined the importance of raw materials. Coal, iron and oil he regarded as the bases of power which in turn created wealth. He pointed out that countries that possess coal, iron and oil, could acquire markets by armed force, and economically dominate other nations.

Science itself does this by the use of energy; electricity powers our computers, it enables us to play electronic games of a kind not dreamed of fifty years ago, it can provide the power to enable us to listen to music in near perfection or to carry our chosen entertainment in our pockets. The Internet is the world's cheapest, most accessible encyclopaedia and product brochure. Electricity enables us to watch sporting or cultural events broadcast from the other side of the world. We can see our politicians argue, debate and attempt to persuade us. We can watch wars as they unfold. Perhaps most important of all, we can see massive tragedies, affecting one person or thousands of people, in all their horror.

We can have illnesses cured, which were incurable a few years ago. We have eradicated some diseases and made others, once fatal, curable. We can extend life and extend quality of life, all by the use of science and energy.

Cheap oil enables us to travel virtually wherever we want. We can drive to the other side of the country on good roads and in reliable cars. We can fly across oceans in safety for less than an average person earns in four days. We can move food and goods from all over the world cheaply, so that many countries develop a kind of manufacturing or service speciality in very product-specific fields.

Cheap gas enables us to live decently and warmly, to wash our clothes after we have worn them for very short periods. Most people can afford to bath and shower when they want to because the cost factor is not significant to them. Forty years ago, on Friday nights in most parts of the country, ordinary people went through the ritual of the Friday night bath; no family member was allowed to use up all the water and someone experienced in doing so would touch the bare copper of the hot water cylinder to try to establish whether the next person would have a sufficiently warm bath.

Although most of us take copious hot water, central heating, television and the Internet for granted, they are wondrous, important things and add significantly to our lives. One gets used to most things fairly quickly, but one gets used to luxury more quickly than anything else. It is not desirable or feasible to require people to be colder, to bath less or to stop using electricity.

We can, in Russell's language, gratify ourselves almost without limit.

But Russell asserted out that the gratification that science brought came without affecting the nature of man. His comments today seem limited and insular. Today many items of so-called gratification are essential to our existence – such as medicines, surgery and good food, all of which are energy intensive.

Human nature may or may not be changed by this process of endless self-gratification, but eventually humans and their environment will change because almost all the energy produced and consumed is fossil based and creates by-products that will provide endless harm even as they provide ephemeral gratification. Gratification inevitably presents the bill, which must be paid.

In these circumstances we must look to alternative energy sources to provide the gratification and the essentials of living. We should start with the impossible sources.

Next to the ideals of alchemy, the drive for free energy has probably been the most fruitless of humankind's quests. The philosopher's stone of free energy has been the perpetual motion machine. Like the conversion of base metal into gold, the perpetual motion machine only has a use in reality as a means of generating wealth for fraudsters operating against the gullible.

In many ways the traditional sources of energy will become, as time goes by, undesirable and unfeasible. There is much doubt about how much oil remains to be extracted from the earth. Supplies seem to be plentiful but things are not always as they appear. Similarly, coal resources must be finite. But regardless of the extent of all fossil fuel supplies, until the energy can be extracted from it without releasing carbon dioxide and other pollutants, burning fossil fuel will always be undesirable because it is environmentally harmful. The significance of environmentally harmful activity is not that it destroys some environments but that it ultimately destroys all environments and thus leaves us no place to live.

The newest large source of energy is that created by nuclear power. In its creation the processes, provided they are rigorously controlled, are benign. The by-product is the problem. It is not possible to know that in, say, five hundred years we shall be able to contain the by-product successfully. Five hundred years is a very long time in history and as civilisations have regressed and forgotten technologies and practices of the past, we cannot be confident that they will retain the skills and desires needed to control the nuclear fuel by-product five hundred years in the future.

We can turn to biomass and similar forms of renewable energy. We think that the case for biomass is unconvincing. Burning any combustible substance creates carbon dioxide and the fact that the biomass may be renewed does not mean that we are placed in a better position. It seems that it would be far better to leave vegetation in place so that it can absorb carbon dioxide through the photosynthesis of plants and only burn it when it is no longer able to do this.

Wind energy is a form that many people hope will provide some solution to the problem of providing clean energy. A landscape covered with wind farms appears unusual and to some people unpleasant. We think that a prospect of wind farms stretching as far as the eye can see is no less intrusive than a landscape covered with traditional power stations together with their massive cooling towers. The windmills are sometimes noisier than we would like them to be and sometimes spoil pleasant views. These are important but not critical considerations as wind farms generate their power in a largely beneficial manner.

There are three more important considerations that apply to wind power. First, when they are combined in wind farms, windmills generate their power away from the places where the energy is to be used. This inevitably means that there will be a massive loss of power in transmission. Secondly, and perhaps more significantly, because a wind generator has many moving parts it is necessary to maintain them continually and this can be expensive, both financially and in the consumption of energy. Thirdly, for an environmental benefit to be achieved we should be sure that the energy used in the manufacture of the wind turbine is substantially less that the energy that it will generate, over its useful lifetime. This is not always the case and some turbines recover the energy expended in their manufacture and installation, only over a time span equivalent to their useful life.

We have seen that ocean thermal power and tidal sources are unlikely to provide a solution to our problems and that heat pumps, while useful, are not cost effective and are unlikely to become so. Further, heat pumps are usually noisy and, as such, not always desired by residential occupiers.

Photovoltaic power (PV) is highly thought of by the Government, but as a source that needs to be improved for future use, not as a source that is viable today. The Government have made £20 million available as at March 2002 as grant contributions to PV installations. Even with the grant all present day PV installations are very expensive and inefficient. Between ten and twenty square meters of PV installation will provide an average home with between 30 and 65% of its electricity. However electricity is the substantially smallest part of a household's energy bill because most energy is expended in gas consumption for space and water heating.

Even if vast economies of scale were possible and the price of PV could be reduced by 80% there would be some major disadvantages in PV. PV produces direct current electricity. We use alternating current and the DC electricity needs to be converted into AC electricity by means of an expensive inverter. In the process there are current conversion losses of between 7 and 12%. PV is by its very nature somewhat fragile. It is unlikely to be robust and results of accelerated aging tests are inconclusive. It is also fairly easily prevented from generating power if a small part of the installation becomes covered.

PV probably recovers the energy used in its manufacture after around seven years and although the manufacturers claim a life expectancy of 20 years these claims have yet to be demonstrated.

This then leaves us to consider the contribution that solar collectors can make. Even though some installations heat water only, water heating can be a far more expensive constituent of the average household budget than its electricity costs. In the United Kingdom the shortness of daylight in winter means that there is unlikely to be enough light to generate 100% of a family's hot water needs, but the 70-80% that a good solar water heating installation can still give makes this form of energy economically viable.

Solar collectors are made of readily recyclable materials – copper, aluminium and glass. Indeed, if the recycling facilities were available we could manufacture collectors wholly from recycled materials.

Solar collectors are proven to be long lasting, provided that they are made by reliable manufacturers and correctly installed. The earliest vacuum tubes made over 30 years ago are still producing heat. The first flat panels made by ThermoSolar 28 years ago are also still producing heat efficiently, and since then manufacturing methods have vastly improved.

Many people voice aesthetic objections to collectors being mounted on roofs. They say that they look unsightly and intrusive. Of course, there is a natural conservatism that seems to apply itself to people's views about architecture and building design. We like what we are used to. Doubtless similar views were expressed when chimneys made their first appearance, in eleventh century England. Solar collectors have not been around as long as chimneys but they have been in existence since 1767, when the Swiss scientist Horace de Saussure built the world's first solar collector. By 1895 30% of the homes in Pasadena were fitted with solar water heating systems.

It is cheap coal and oil, not the aesthetic objections, that have delayed the further expansion of the market for solar water heating until now.

Solar collectors can also provide the kind of ambient heat which, in Europe, has been successfully harnessed to under floor and in wall heating installations. Under floor heating by circulating hot water through a special system of two multicore pipes (which allow for the different coefficients of expansion, thus preventing pipe noise and movement) has yet to be undertaken in a large way in this country. Much better public information would resolve this problem, in particular the explanation that, with all solar energy installations, the secret is to either use the energy as you collect it, or else store it. Just as a hot water installation powered by solar energy works more efficiently with a larger storage cylinder, so a very large storage vessel is need to power solar heating.

Ideally, the storage vessel should be not less than 1000 litres – around eight and a half times the size of an average cylinder. Homes with basements can prove ideal for this technology, unless they are arranged like a traditional Georgian home on five or six floors. In order to get the best advantage from solar central heating it is necessary for our building design to change, to incorporate a store at basement level and to design roofs with built-in collectors facing south. As we have mentioned elsewhere, loft space can also be used.

It is an interesting speculation that a simple way to enable the United Kingdom to meet its Kyoto emission targets would be to require solar collectors, not PV, to be installed on every new roof and in every redevelopment. In these circumstances the Government's current obsession with PV technology seems misplaced. There is no doubt that the PV lobby has some powerful voices; the oil companies Shell and BP both manufacture PV cells. A former Government adviser runs one PV Company. By contrast the solar hot water industry is not well connected.

The real problem from which we suffer is that plumbing-related activities are often the Cinderella trade. In this country we still sell and install more non-condensing boilers than condensing boilers, by a long way. A non-condensing boiler is regarded in Germany and Holland as akin to Stone Age technology; why do we permit them here when cost and global warming are such important issues?

There is no government or official system of monitoring and testing solar products. There is scant governmental information available about them. There is no proper encouragement for training heating and ventilation engineers in solar technologies, although we have been encouraged by the new generation of young engineers, knowledgeable and keen to use their skills in an environmentally responsible manner.

Bertrand Russell was not speaking about global warming in his essay on "Icarus, or the Future of Science". Russell was a pacifist; he drew an analogy, which we, in our present circumstances, would, however, appreciate in environmental terms:

"Some people think that we keep our rooms too hot for health, others that we keep them too cold. If this were a political question, one party would maintain that the best temperature is the absolute zero, the other that it is the melting point of iron. Those who maintained any intermediate position would be abused as timorous time-servers, concealed agents of the other side, men

who ruined the enthusiasm of a sacred cause by tepid appeals to mere reason. Any man who had the courage to say that our rooms ought to be neither very hot nor very cold would be abused by both parties, and probably shot in No Man's Land. Possibly some day politics may become more rational, but so far there is not the faintest indication of a change in this direction."

Russell concluded in his essay that science threatens to cause the destruction of our civilisation, and although he did not write from an environmental perspective, his words are beginning to ring true in the sense that science has enabled us to use energy as intensively and as greedily as we do.

Russell wrote his essay in response to an essay by J. B. S. Haldane called "Daedalus, or, Science and the Future". Here is Haldane's vision of the future created by the benefits of science:

"The country will be covered with rows of metallic windmills working electric motors, which in their turn supply current at a very high voltage to great electric mains. At suitable distances, there will be great power stations where during windy weather the surplus power will be used for the electrolytic decomposition of water into oxygen and hydrogen. These gasses will be lique-fied, and stored in vast vacuum jacketed reservoirs, probably sunk in the ground. If these reservoirs are sufficiently large, the loss of liquid due to leakage inwards of heat will not be great; thus the proportion evaporating daily from a reservoir 100 yards square by 60 feet deep would not be 1/1000 of that lost from a tank measuring two feet each way. In times of calm, the gasses will be recombined in explosion motors working dynamos which produce electrical energy once more, or more probably in oxi-dation cells.... These huge reservoirs of liquefied gasses will enable wind energy to be stored, so that it can be expended for industry, transportation, heating and lighting, as desired. ... Energy will be as cheap in one part of the country as another, so that industry will be greatly decentralized; and that no smoke or ash will be produced."

Haldane's vision seems today a curious mixture of reality and idealism. Russell's vision is frightening because he lacks confidence in humankind's intrinsic collective ability to act moderately and properly.

There is no single solution to our problem of global warming. We will have to try all technologies and combine them, so that we draw as much energy from non-carbon-releasing sources as possible. We need the best technology, the best processes and the best scientists to help us to maintain our life styles without poisoning the planet; if that cannot be done we shall have to modify our lifestyles. This modification may amount to no more than some intrusions on buildings and landscapes if we act now. If we delay, then our lifestyles and those of our children will perish altogether.

As we have seen, predicting the future is a hazardous business. It is safer to concentrate on what we should be doing, and having set out the rules, let the future take care of itself. We would suggest that the following points are worthy of consideration:

1. We need to have a universal statement of environmental obligations, which should be adopted by all states, organisations institutions and people. The statement should be one of principle and should not refer to any other issues, however laudable or important they are perceived to be.

2. We should make the polluter pay not only the clean up costs but also damages for loss of amenity. It is wrong for anyone to profit from anti-social behaviour; we have laws prohibiting criminals from profiting from their crimes and we should have similar rules, preventing, for example, corporations profiting from pollution-causing activities.

3. We should do what we can immediately; this means more taxation on energy that is carbon-releasing and more incentives for solar and wind power.

4. We should recognise that investing in any "green" technology requires a householder to release a large capital sum; the householder will get pay back and then free energy, but paying out a large capital sum means that the householder loses the security of having it for emergencies. We have to address this.

5. We should fit solar water heating in all social housing; this solves two problems with one solution – fuel poverty is greatly reduced and the carbon issue is addressed.

6. We should require that real energy saving "green" technologies – solar water and space heating for example – are installed

where suitable in all new build homes and all refurbished homes.

7. We should provide permanent Council Tax reductions to homes that have solar installations, while increasing Council Tax on homes without them. This would be fiscally neutral and would substantially reduce concerns over long pay back.

8. We should look at our methods of funding schools and hospitals; they have no incentive to save income, by installing solar, if it means that they have to spend capital. They will have enough money to keep the institution in fossil fuel, but not a penny to avoid using fossil fuel.

9. We have to address the short-term requirements of industry. Many large commercial organisations have told Genersys that they will only consider solar power if there will be a three year payback. The rules and tax system should be changed to make an investment by the local supermarket or factory in solar power much more likely.

10. We should name and shame polluters much more than we do; pollution and contributing to global warming are just about the most antisocial behaviour it is possible to commit and it should be recognised as such.

Icarus was the son of a scientist, Daedalus. Icarus wore the wings of wax and feathers that his father made, and flew. He became so enthralled with his ability to fly that he failed to heed the warning of his father, Daedalus the scientist. Gratifying himself with the thrill of his wings of wax, Icarus forgot to keep away from the sun. His wings melted and he perished in the Aegean Sea.

Our scientists are warning us about the danger of continued fossil fuel consumption. If we ignore their warnings we shall perish, like the Icarus of legend.

Endword

I am grateful to Genersys for giving me the opportunity to have the last word in their specially commissioned book about energy in the United Kingdom.

Since Genersys was formed I have met many people concerned with the environment who really understand the issues that are critical. I have much admiration for many local authority personnel who can see how, for example, solar power can not only address environmental issues but also alleviate fuel poverty. I have met environmentally dedicated professionals such as architects, surveyors and engineers. I have met people from many countries; they often bring a different perspective to these issues and frequently bring expertise and solutions to our problems.

It has become clear to me that environmental issues can only really be addressed by taking a mainly commercial approach, but that inevitably requires some basic rethinking of three principles.

First, consumers consume. That is the essence of all environmental problems and those who regard the protection of the consumers' right to consume, as more important than the consumers' obligations to the environment, have somewhat lost the plot. I include not only consumer organisations but also all those consumer entertainments of television and the radio.

Second, built in obsolescence has no place in modern manufacturing. Quality should be paramount. Quality should be rewarded and regarded as vital because in the long run, (and in environmental terms the long run is a very short period indeed) high quality saves consumption.

Third, government should give a clear lead in these issues. At the moment, governments are not leading. The homeowner is faced with confusing signals from government. There is no clear central message.

No one sets up a business in order to save the environment. If one consequence of a business's operation is to help save the environment, then those working in such businesses are the true eco-warriors of the twenty-first century.

Robert Kyriakides
CEO, Genersys plc, London, July 2002

Index